FIFTY SHADES
OF BLACK

FIFTY SHADES
OF BLACK

Arthur Black

To Janie, Jimbo
Rudy & Molly
Happy Thanksgiving 2013!

Douglas & McIntyre

1 2 3 4 5 — 17 16 15 14 13

Douglas and McIntyre (2013) Ltd.
P.O. Box 219
Madeira Park, BC, Canada V0N 2H0
www.douglas-mcintyre.com

Printed and bound in Canada

Edited by Margaret Tessman
Text design by Mary White
Cover photograph by Howard Fry

Cataloguing data available from Library and Archives Canada
ISBN 978-1-77162-019-2 (cloth)
ISBN 978-1-77162-020-8 (ebook)

We gratefully acknowledge financial support from the Government of Canada through the Canada Book Fund and the Canada Council for the Arts, and from the Province of British Columbia through the BC Arts Council and the Book Publishing Tax Credit.

To Cathy Ward,
without whom this book would have been called . . .
God knows what.

Contents

Introduction

I'm walking down the main street of my home town when Cathy Ward, a delightful woman of my acquaintance, brazenly accosts me.

"Hey, Arthur," she says, "I've got the title for your next book."

I resist the urge to sweep her into my arms, bend her backwards and smother her with Sheik of Araby style kisses. Book titles are my personal albatross, my hand-hewn Sisyphean boulder, the monkey that grins over my shoulder, securely saddled to my back.

My personal *bête noire*, if you will.

Here's the deal. I've written fifteen books; they all have my name in the title. They include *Looking Blackward, Basic Black, Back to Black, Pitch Black, Black Gold, A Chip Off the Old Bla* . . . you get the idea. The point is, what started out as a clever gimmick graduated to tricky, then burdensome and finally nightmarish. I had run out of ways to work "black" into my titles. What to do? Start a contest? Engage an advertising agency? Quit writing books?

None of the above, because one fine day, strolling down the main street of my home town Cathy Ward buttonholed me and said "You should call it *Fifty Shades of Black*."

Bingo!

Later, someone asked me if I was worried that somebody might get *Fifty Shades of Black* mixed up with that other *Fifty Shades of* . . . book. You know, the one that features whips and chains and handcuffs and riding crops and that, at last count, has sold seventy-five million copies worldwide. What if several hundred thousand readers bought my book by mistake?

I replied that naturally I was terrified of the prospect, but willing to take a chance.

—ARTHUR BLACK

Extra! Extra! Read All About Me!

HEY! MY NAME IS ARTHUR BLACK! I HAVE A NEW BOOK OUT! IT'S CALLED *FIFTY SHADES OF BLACK*! IT'S PUBLISHED BY DOUGLAS & MCINTYRE! IT'S HILARIOUS! YOU SHOULD BUY A COPY! RIGHT NOW!!!

Please forgive my un-Canadian pushiness. I've just come from a workshop for writers entitled "How to Be Your Own Publicist." Here is what I learned:

1. I am not just a writer; I am a brand.
2. I need to max out my credit cards and start travelling all over Canada to "meet and greet" with bookstore owners from Haida Gwaii to Joe Batt's Arm.
3. I need to chat up bookstore customers, subtly steering them by the elbow over to the Canadian Humour section and asking them if they see any names that look familiar, nudge, nudge.
4. I need to attend booksellers' conventions in a rented tux and throw myself at the feet of booksellers and publishers' agents.
5. I need to enlist fifty friends and/or family members to talk up my book and strong-arm local bookstores into featuring it in their windows.
6. I need to join Facebook, create a blog, master Twitter and

overhaul my website to reach the teeming masses who would all buy my book if only I tweeted, blogged and Facebooked about it.

It was at about this point in the workshop that I wanted to stand up and shout that I would prefer a colonoscopy by Roto-Rooter to engaging in any of the aforementioned stunts.

I didn't stand up and say that of course, because (a) I'm Canadian and (b) dammit, that is not writerly behaviour. Writers are detached. Aloof. Introverted. Okay—shy and awkward. We don't wear lampshades at parties or dazzle the crowds with our tango moves. We aren't cool. We trend geekwards.

Hey, that's why we became writers in the first place. Do you think if we could dance or do stand-up or be otherwise socially dynamic we'd be wasting our time making scribbles on paper or pecking away on laptops?

We certainly don't do it for the money. Do you know what the average annual salary is for a Canadian writer? Two thousand seven hundred and twenty-five bucks. (Okay, I made that up—but statistics show that 80 percent of all statistics are made up on the spot.)

The very attraction of being a writer (aside from the princely sums you haul down) is that you don't have to go to an office to do it. Writers may be underpaid, but on the plus side, we're pretty much totally ignored. We can write in our pyjamas at the kitchen table with three days of stubble on our chins or our hair in curlers. Writers don't have to worry about the boss barging in on them, contributions to the office birthday fund or showing up late for work.

As for the downside, well, nobody ever put it better than Bennett Cerf, one of the founding publishers of Random House:

"Bunyan spent a year in prison, Coleridge was a drug addict, Poe was an alcoholic, Marlowe was killed by a man he was trying to stab. Pope took a large sum of money to keep a woman's name out of a vicious satire and then wrote it so she could be recognized anyway. Chatterton killed himself, Somerset Maugham was so unhappy in his final thirty years that he longed for death . . . do you still want to be a writer?"

The answer is, oddly enough, yeah. Being a writer isn't so much an occupation as a condition. An itch that needs to be scratched.

You want to be rich? Be a hockey player. Famous? Invent a cure for baldness. Powerful? Go suck up to somebody in Stephen Harper's office.

The writing business isn't about any of those things—unless your name is Bill Shakespeare or J.K. Rowling. For the rest of us, motivation is very simple. As a Greek fella named Epictetus put it a couple of thousand years ago: "If you wish to write, write."

Oh, and don't forget to advertise!

HEY! MY NAME IS ARTHUR BLACK! I HAVE A NEW BOOK OUT! IT'S CALLED *FIFTY SHADES OF BLACK*! IT'S PUBLISHED BY DOUGLAS & MCINTYRE! IT'S HILARIOUS! YOU SHOULD BUY A COPY! RIGHT NOW!!!

Caution: Klutz on the Loose

I'm thinking of taking chainsaw lessons.

Which is weird because I like chainsaws the way I like underarm rash. If there's one sound I hate more than chalk scrawking on a blackboard, the blatting of an amateur bagpiper or the yowl of an alley cat in heat, it's the sound of a chainsaw roaring to life.

And yet, and yet . . . there's this thirty-foot arbutus in my backyard that just hit the dirt and is begging to be bucked up into firewood. Yeah, I suppose I could do it with a swede saw. I could trim the front lawn with toenail clippers too, but I'm not going to.

The undeniable saving grace about chainsaws is: they work. Slicker than a Karen Kain pas de deux, a Christopher Plummer soliloquy. Roberto Luongo on a good night.

More important, I've got a chainsaw maestra living just up island from me. Her name is Mearnie Summers and she not only gives chainsaw lessons, she does chainsaw art. And I don't mean that hokey bear cub out of a tree trunk stuff—I mean real art. And crafts. Like mobiles and tables and chairs.

You might think that a Husqvarna or a Stihl chainsaw is a relatively unsubtle paintbrush for an artist to employ, but Mearnie brings a delicate touch to her work—which she claims has next to nothing to do with her anyway. She doesn't impose her vision on the chunk of cherry or cedar or arbutus she's working on. She claims she just "goes the way the wood goes."

It figures Mearnie would say something shrubby like that because she's about as typical as Salt Springers get—which is to say highly untypical. In previous incarnations she ran construction crews in the Interior, floated barges along the coast and ran the general store in Surge Narrows. She was also the first woman to circumnavigate Vancouver Island by sail, crewed a thirty-two-footer to Tahiti and back, gave dance lessons and played pro baseball in the States. So teaching greenhorns like me how to chainsaw timber is as easy for her as, well, falling off a log.

Or should be.

Someone should maybe forewarn Mearnie that as a student I have an MA in Advanced Klutz. When it comes to things mechanical I make Woody Allen look like Mikhail Baryshnikov. As for mechanical things with teeth, I'm not even allowed to operate the electric can opener at home.

I mentioned my misgivings to my pals down at the coffee house. "Don't be ridiculous," one of them scoffed. "Chainsaw's just another tool. There's nothing to it. A five-year-old child could run a chainsaw and never get a scratch."

Maybe he's right. I'm just overreacting. But I'd feel a lot more confident if my pal's nickname wasn't Stumpy.

Ownly the Loanly

You ever been dead broke? Neither have I. Oh, back when I was
younger and stupider I received my share of snarky phone calls
and envelopes plastered with PAST DUE in fluorescent capitals. But
I never had to shinny down a flophouse drainpipe in the middle of
the night and I've never answered a knock to find a tall dark stranger
named Guido lounging against the door frame cracking his knuckles
and inquiring about "the vig."

It's not because I'm wealthy (ask my bank manager) or fiscally
nimble. My entire economic strategy boils down to a motto espoused
by the Dickens character Mr. Micawber: "Annual income twenty
pounds, annual expenditure nineteen pounds nineteen and six, result
happiness. Annual income twenty pounds, annual expenditure twenty
pounds nought and six, result misery."

Sounds crude and simplistic, but it works at least as well as the
collected wisdom of Goldman Sachs.

All debt is relative. As some wag once said, if you owe the bank a
hundred dollars, you've got a problem. If you owe the bank a million
dollars, the bank's got a problem. Me? I owe some guy in a Moroccan
village twenty cents. It's not really a problem but it's a debt I'll never
forget.

Decades ago, as a teenager hitchhiking across North Africa, I
found myself stranded one day in a tiny town in the Atlas Mountains.
What passed for the bank was closed for Ramadan, ATMs were as yet

undreamed of and I was down to my very last dirham—a small coin worth something less than two bits. Accommodation was no problem as long as I didn't mind smelling goatish—but I was hungry. Very hungry. Around sundown I found a hole-in-the-wall restaurant that sold nothing but stew. Price per bowl, one dirham. I lined up with a sketchy-looking string of customers, nervously fingering my last coin. I arrived at the stew cauldron at the same moment as a scowling, djellaba-clad Tuareg. He glowered at me; I motioned for him to go ahead, even as my stomach voted otherwise. The stranger disdainfully swept ahead, got his stew and left without a thank you or a backward glance. When I got my bowlful and offered to pay, my coin was refused. The stew dispenser indicated with a flick of his head that Mr. Nasty had paid my tab.

I can still taste that stew. And I still think of the stranger I owe for it.

Being in debt isn't always just about the money. Early in his career, comedian Jackie Gleason had an engagement at a burlesque house in Atlantic City. The gig ended, the cheque from the burlesque house bounced and Gleason couldn't pay his room and board. Intending to skip town, Gleason packed up his clothes, lowered his suitcase out a window to a waiting accomplice then waddled casually past the reception desk wearing nothing but bathing trunks and carrying a towel. "Just off to the beach," he assured the landlady.

Years later when Gleason was flush, guilt propelled him back to the boarding house to make good on his debt.

The landlady shrieked at the sight of him.

"Oh, my Lord!" she cried. "We thought you'd drowned."

Fan Mail Welcome;
Clipping, Not So Much

There are three cardinal rules I try to follow in life:

1. Never argue with airport security staff. (You won't win and you might miss your flight.)
2. Always answer "No" to the question "Do these slacks make my hips look big?"
3. Always answer your fan mail promptly.

Okay, the last one's easy. When it comes to fan mail I ain't exactly Lady Gaga. It's not like I have to hire a fleet of secretaries to deal with the cataracts of emails and letters flooding in, but I do get some. And I do my very best to answer it the same day. Why, you ask? Well, I'm Canadian, eh? It's the polite thing to do. Recently, however, I learned an even more compelling reason for responding quickly to fan mail.

Justin Bieber.

Not long ago, police in New Mexico announced that Dana Martin, a three-time loser and convicted killer, had arranged—from his jail cell—to pay associates to castrate Justin Bieber with hedge clippers.

Interestingly, it was not the quality of Mr. Bieber's musical offerings that Mr. Martin objected to, nor was it the pop star's goofy hairstyle.

It was the fact that Mr. Martin's many fan letters to the pop star had gone unanswered.

Because of the perceived snub, Mr. Martin was reportedly prepared to pay three hit men five thousand dollars for delivery of "the Bieber package." Specifically, twenty-five hundred dollars per testicle.

When it comes to answering fan mail, you can't be too careful. Or too prompt.

I worked in radio for many years and for some of those years my fan mail reached me with a curious time delay built in. I noticed that the envelopes (this was in pre-email times) all bore the inscription "Forwarded." Turns out there was a gentleman in my neighbour-hood who bore the exceedingly vulnerable moniker of Athol Black. Fans (friendly and otherwise) would call Directory Assistance to get my mailing address, the operator would say, "I have a Mr. Athol Black listed," and the fan would say "Yeah—that's the one I want! The ath-hole who talks onna radio alla time."

Which raises the question: what to do with crank mail?

For me it depends on the virulence level. If someone writes to tell me that I'm an inconsiderate, illiterate lazy slob who's ignorant, opin-ionated and about as funny as a root canal, I write back acknowledging that my next-door neighbours, my grade six teacher, my children and my wife wholeheartedly concur. If, however, they write that I'm a treasonous, illegitimate fascist who ought to be castrated with hedge clippers, I write back to say the RCMP have asked for a home address so they can come over for a chat.

Happily, most fan mail is not so sulphurous or mean-spirited. We are Canadians after all, which means (outside of hockey arenas and Normandy beaches) most of us are friendly, generous and polite to a fault. That's why when people write to me, even to disagree with something I've written, they usually do so in a genteel and civilized manner. I appreciate that. Over the years, many lively correspondences and more than a few friendships have blossomed because I faithfully answer my fan mail.

As a matter of fact, this afternoon I'm off to have coffee with someone I've never met who contacted me by mail. We've arranged to meet at a coffee shop downtown.

Mind you, if a stranger shows up lugging a pair of hedge clippers, I'm going out the back door.

'Tis the Season of the Chrome-Dome

Allow me to introduce myself: I am a bald male.

Not bald as in "bald eagle." (The bird got a bad rap. *Balde* is an antique word meaning "white"; so-called bald eagles actually get to spend their entire lives with a fine, full head of handsome . . . well, feathers.)

I digress.

I am, as I say, a mature male *Homo sapiens* whose upper deck is shorn of shrubbery, devoid of pelt, a filament-free zone. I did not arrive at this state overnight but rather gradually, like a mighty oak shedding its leaves. And not in one season: over several years.

I have to confess, going bald wasn't much fun. I grew up in the Elvis Era, when any young buck worth a dab of Brylcreem sported a poofy ducktail and a greasy pompadour imposing enough to qualify as a traffic hazard. To a man, we dreamed of owning a car, being a rock star and getting laid. We did not entertain the notion of going bald.

So actually going bald was somewhat traumatic. Ah, but BEING bald? That's been a piece of cake. Let me enumerate a few of the advantages:

Economy: I don't spend a dime on shampoos, conditioners, revitalizers, tints, dyes, mousse or gels. You won't find electric hair dryers or straighteners or epilators in my bathroom. Which of course means . . .

Less Bathroom Time: Know how I comb my hair for an important event? With a damp washcloth. One pass and phhhhht!—I'm cleared for takeoff.

The BS Factor: Here are two truisms.

Number One: There are, in fact, attractive-looking people out there who actually care whether their partners have "great hair" or not.

Number Two: You don't want to know them.

Think for a moment about the intellectual depth of anyone who judges anyone else on the basis of what's growing north of their eyebrows.

That's not how you judge a person; that's how you judge a lawn.

Being bald frees you from the time-consuming process of buying drinks or dinner for someone and wasting an evening discovering through conversation how vapid and superficial he or she is.

Being bald is like having a social Get Out of Jail Free card.

And this just in (literally): a study conducted by researchers at the University of Pennsylvania's Wharton School concludes that bald men are actually perceived as more powerful, more manly and even taller than men with hair.

Well, correction—not men who are merely bald—men who actually shave their heads. "The basic finding is that people view the shaved head as a powerful look," says the study author, Albert Mannes.

Uh-huh. And what about guys on their way to going bald, with wisps and tufts and hair horseshoes around their head?

Uh-uh.

"Men with thinning hair were viewed as least favourable," says Mannes.

So there you have it, my little studlings. You can have a polished pate like Patrick Stewart or a hirsute noggin like Justin Trudeau—but nothing in between.

Personally, and speaking as a guy who has occupied both pedestals, I'd get out the BIC disposable if I were you. Being bald is easier, more hygienic, cheaper and, if the Pennsylvania University study is correct, the more virile way to go.

Nobody said it better than the British writer Logan Pearsall Smith: "There is more felicity on the far side of baldness than young men can possibly imagine."

Amen to that. Eat your heart out, hairballs.

Aging Jubilantly

I am not a coot.

Neither am I a geezer, a buzzard, gramps or old-timer—and woe betide the wet-behind-the-ears johnny-come-lately who tries to brand me with the repugnant "senior citizen" or worse yet "golden ager."

Curmudgeon? Sometimes, for sure. Elder? I suppose, though it sounds a little priggish and highfalutin to my ear.

To tell you the truth, I don't much like any of the terms customarily draped over Those of Us Who Have Attained a Certain Measure of Maturity.

Except for one. I think I could handle being labelled a *jubilado*.

It's pronounced "hoo-bee-LAH-dough" and it's what Spaniards call their retirees. In English it means pretty much what it looks like—"jubilant one."

Oh—and heads up. It's defiantly sex specific. Guys are *jubilados*; girls are *jubiladas*. Deal with it.

And truly, why not "jubilant ones"? Most of us who get to this age bracket are bedecked and festooned with reasons to celebrate. We are less encumbered than we've ever been in our lives. The kids are grown and unleashed; the mortgage, if not paid off, is under control. We wear what we choose, get up when we please and no longer give a fig about rush hour commutes, layoffs, pro- or demotions or the emotional ups and downs of the psycho boss in the corner office. We can choose to watch the sunrise or plump the pillow over our head; walk the dog or slurp margaritas in a hammock; spend the afternoon with a good book or catch a baseball game on the tube.

What's not to be jubilant about? Alas, our society discourages jubilation in its jubilados. We're treated more like hockey players past their prime. There's a sense we've been put out to pasture, sent home with a gold Timex and a permanent time out. We've done our stretch and nothing further is expected of us. We can sit back, relax and fade into the wallpaper.

Well, screw that.

I choose to be a jubilado. I'm going to make noise, dance up a storm, kick up some dust, raise a little hell and generally make some whoopie. Why not? It feels good to be a jubilado.

Anybody can get older. Hell, boulders do that. The trick is to age in style. Some choose to do it by diversion—two weeks in Maui, a few rounds of golf, tickets to see the Jets or Leonard Cohen, a shopping spree through Holt Renfrew or Lululemon—they all make you feel good, if only for a little while.

Others turn their focus outward, embracing volunteerism, philanthropy or the simple care and nurturing of friends and family.

Still others go out and buy themselves a flamboyant red hat. Aging well doesn't have to be a 180-degree U-turn. It can be a simple shift in your colour spectrum. Jenny Joseph showed us that when she wrote a hit poem entitled "Warning, When I Am an Old Woman I Shall Wear Purple."

Take your choice and fill your boots. But do it joyously, jubilantly.

And me? You can colour me purple. In a cherry-red Stetson.

And I Mean That Sincerely

Number one on my bucket list this week: to track down whoever it is who runs the US website CareerCast.com. Purpose: to corner the doofus and give his or her head a good shake.

CareerCast has just published its list of the best and worst jobs of 2012. I had to read it twice to be sure I wasn't having an acid flashback from the '60s.

According to CareerCast, two of the best jobs you can have are "actuary" or "financial planner."

Actuary? Best job??? Do you think the folks at CareerCast actuary know what an actuary does? My dictionary defines "actuary" as a person who compiles and analyzes statistics and uses them to calculate insurance risks and premiums.

That's a best job, huh?

Perhaps it's because I'm still carrying grade 10 algebra, but I would rather be trapped in a stalled elevator with a case of the trots than spend a nanosecond sitting at a desk toiling as an actuary.

As for being a financial planner, let's see now . . . would that be like filling out your income tax form FOREVER?

CareerCast's list of worst jobs is equally exasperating. The absolute worst job, they say is "lumberjack"—what Western Canadians call "logger."

Well, I'd call it dangerous, for sure, and there's no question that felling trees in the forest is a strenuous way to make a buck. But worst job in the world? Do you think the folks at CareerCast.com ever unclogged a septic field? Dodged a rodeo bull? Crawled on their bellies through a rat-infested attic?

I've never been a logger but I have been a dairy hand and a restaurant waiter—and those jobs also make CareerCast's worst job list.

Balderdash. I've worked at both those occupations and, aside from crummy tippers and the occasional cow tail in the eye, found plenty to enjoy about them.

As somebody once said, anything can be a dead-end job if you're a dead-end guy.

I'd be happy to simply dismiss CareerCast's dismal listings with a shrug if it weren't for the job they've slotted as the tenth worst—"broadcaster."

Now hold on just a minute.

I worked behind a microphone at CBC Radio for thirty years and I can tell you it was easily one of the best jobs I ever had.

Well, think about it: no heavy lifting, all the tea or coffee you can drink, a roof over your head, a company computer with unlimited Internet access, free review copies from book publishers and the odd complimentary ticket to a hockey game, a movie or a stage show.

No dress code of course—it's radio, nobody can see you. I could read the six o'clock news wearing a Bozo the Clown nose and a purple tutu and no one would be the wiser.

Plus, all the training you really need for the job is usually under your belt by grade four. Can you read? You're hired.

Okay, it's not quite that simple—but close. As my first radio mentor explained to me in a plummy Shakespearian basso profundo: "My boy, the most important quality you can have as a radio broadcaster is sincerity."

Then he gripped my hand firmly, looked deep into my eyes and added, "Once you can fake that, you've got it made."

Broadcasting one of the ten worst jobs? Nonsense. It's the best job ever.

And I mean that sincerely.

Big Bully? Big Deal

Runt: n. 1. A variety of domestic pigeon. 2. The dead stump of a tree. 3. Any animal which is unusually small compared with others of its kind.

I come from a family of two girls and two boys and I was unquestionably the runt of the litter.

Oh, I wasn't feeble or sickly as an infant, but I was . . . small—and slower to develop than most of my kiddie colleagues. By the time I hit puberty my classmates were already sporting sideburns and breasts (each to his or her own, you understand). Public school was unrelieved misery. I never won any ribbons on Field Day and I stayed on the bench at school dances—mostly because all the girls were at least a head taller than me. Naturally, I sucked at sports. When the captains chose up sides for baseball games I was usually the last pick.

"Okay, you have to take Black," the opposing captain would say.

I was definitely low man on the totem pole. The skinny pup on the hind teat. The runt of the litter.

It was the best thing that ever happened to me.

Being a runt reveals social Darwinism at its most cold-blooded. Runts are automatically at the bottom of the pecking order and they have to think fast if they expect to survive. They have to hone their hearing to stay out of the way of their more robust siblings. They have to sharpen their vision and sense of smell to snatch the scraps before the Big Guys get them. Runts have to develop a kind of radar to be able to analyze situations more quickly.

Otherwise they're toast.

I remember when I was maybe nine or ten years old, rafting in a creek swollen by spring runoff. I was poling along the creek doing fine until Timmy Fermier, a big kid, took a huge leap from the creek bank and jumped on the raft with me. Not good. The raft began to settle ominously in the water, which began to creep up my boots. Inspired, I faked hysteria. "WE'RE SINKING! WE'RE SINKING!" I shrieked. "WE'RE GONNA DROWN!"

It worked. Timmy freaked and leapt into the creek (which was only about three feet deep). Naturally, when he abandoned ship, the raft bobbed up and I poled serenely to shore.

True, he beat me up later—but at least I didn't get wet.

Being a runt made me learn other survival skills. If Timmy Fermier was the bullmastiff in the motley mob of mutts I hung around with, I was the Jack Russell terrier: yappy and annoying but fleet of foot and an artful dodger when the other dogs turned mean.

In *The Brothers Karamazov*, the Russian writer Fyodor Dostoevsky wrote: "Schoolboys are a merciless race, individually they are angels, but together, especially in schools, they are often merciless."

It's true. And it's a lesson every schoolboy runt learns early and remembers for the rest of his life. Some runts never get past it and go on to live nervous, stunted lives, shrinking from danger, some of it real but most of it imagined. Others learn to play the hand of cards life dealt them.

As Charles Darwin said: "It is not the strongest of the species that survives, nor the most intelligent that survives. It is the one that is the most adaptable to change."

My all-time favourite runt hero? The skinny little guy, who, legend has it, went for a wilderness hike in the Yukon accompanied by a larger, beefy guide. After a few kilometres they come to a clearing and spy a huge male grizzly on the other side. The bear spots the hikers, gives a gut-shivering roar and begins to gallop across the clearing toward them. "Quick! Take off your jacket and wave it at him!" yells the guide. Instead, the runt shrugs off his backpack, opens the flap and pulls out a pair of running shoes. "Are you crazy?" says the guide. "You can't outrun a grizzly!"

"I don't have to," says the little guy as he sloughs off his heavy boots and slips into the sneakers. "I just have to outrun you."

Memo to Self: Wake Up

Every morning I submit to a dose of physical exercise, deep breathing and forced meditation under the mentorship of my two dogs. It's an hour-plus walk they take me on every day and it is beautiful. Through a rain forest along a salmon creek to the ocean. It's like walking through an Emily Carr or Carol Evans landscape. My walk is, in the ancient sense of the word, a blessing.

And far too often, I ruin it by doing an abidingly stupid thing: I think. I retreat to that hidey-hole in my head to stew in a dog's breakfast of past memories, future plans and other cerebral Post-it Notes, fleeting and meaningless. Sometimes I'll go twenty minutes on autopilot, wake with a start and realize that although my dogs have been sniffing and peering and barking and peeing, I've been elsewhere. I'm still moving, but I haven't seen or heard or smelled a thing for the past quarter mile. What a waste.

Now let me introduce you to a book by a man who is the opposite of all that. The man's name is Adrian Dorst. The book is called *Reflections at Sandhill Creek*. The creek in the title is a small one that empties into Long Beach, up Tofino way. Chances are you'd pass over Sandhill Creek without so much as a sideways glance. But not, I think, after you've seen this book. Adrian Dorst lived near the mouth of the creek for two years and he's lived on and traversed around the Clayoquot Sound area for nearly four decades, taking photos and doing what I so often fail to do: paying attention to the surroundings.

For thirty-five years Dorst hiked along the beaches, watched the sunsets, listened to the waves . . . and took photographs. Everything from mountains in the moonlight to moon snails at low tide; from a delicate blossom of Indian paintbrush in a coastal meadow to a couple of hundred pounds of quizzical cougar stretched along a branch gazing back at the camera.

This book would be worth seeing just for the pictures but it's more than a picture book. Dorst has married the photographs with thoughts. Not his—others. There are quotations from Einstein and Henry Miller; from the I Ching and Aristotle; from Herman Hesse and Bob Dylan. It's eclectic, and it works. Under a panoramic photo of a massive breaker crashing against a rock in Pacific Rim National Park he puts the Buddhist saying "Everything that arises, does its dance and dies." The photograph of the languid cougar—about which animal we are hearing dread warnings on the news almost daily—bears an aphorism from Marie Curie. It reads: "Nothing is to be feared. It is only to be understood."

There is also a photo of a tiny bird, a plover standing amid seashells and facing into the windy grey skies off Stubbs Island.

The caption comes from La Rochefoucauld but it's got my name on it. It reads: "Little is needed to make a wise man happy, but nothing can content a fool."

I'm pretty sure that's what my dogs are trying to tell me every morning.

Male Vanity: It's Inhairited

According to the Guinness World Records, an Indian gentleman by the name of Ram Singh Chauhan has the longest one in the world (4.2 metres if you can believe it). Groucho Marx had a rather splendid attachment and the Oriental mystery-solver Charlie Chan was very well endowed indeed. Hitler? Well, it's no wonder the man was nuts. He had just a stubby little tuftlet about half the length of your pinky finger.

Get your mind out of the gutter, madame—we're talking about the moustache here; a.k.a. soup strainer, cookie duster, Fu Manchu, handlebar, walrus, toothbrush, pencil and, Canada's contribution—the lush and luxuriant Lanny McDonald stable-broom special. Growing a moustache is an unrepentant Man Thing and it's an altar that males have been genuflecting before probably since we bunked down in caves.

For no good reason, as far as I can see. There are few physical affectations more useless than a moustache. Aside from storing toast crumbs and frightening small children, they're not much good for anything.

But don't try to tell that to Selahattin Tulunay. He's a plastic surgeon who practises in Istanbul. Dr. Tulunay specializes in a surgical technique called "follicular unit extraction," which is a fancy way of saying he re-seeds body hair. He plucks healthy hair follicles from one place—say, your back—and replants them in an arid zone. Say . . . above your upper lip.

This does not sound like an operation many North American males would line up for, but Dr. Tulunay does a brisk business in the Middle East, where moustaches—particularly big, bristly, walrus-style moustaches—are serious symbols of virility.

The procedure is painful, unsightly and takes six months to show results. Oh, and it costs about seven thousand dollars per upper lip. Dr. Tulunay is booked solid for months in advance.

According to Andrew Hammond, a journalist based in Saudi Arabia, having a huge, substantial moustache is, well, huge, for Arab males. "Most Arab leaders have moustaches or some form of facial hair. I think culturally it suggests masculinity, wisdom and experience."

The converse is also true. A few years ago militants in Gaza kidnapped an opponent and inflicted on him the most severe and humiliating punishment they could devise, short of death.

They shaved off his moustache.

You want to smear a Middle Eastern man with the worst slander possible? Don't belittle his politics, make fun of his belly or cast aspersions on his family. Just look him in the eye and growl, "A curse be upon your moustache!" When I was a teenager I cursed the place where my moustache wasn't. Long after my pals had sprouted facial hair the area between my nose and my upper lip remained as bare as Senator Duffy's pate.

I rubbed it, I scrubbed it. I slathered on gobfuls of hair restorer and even shaved it, for an old wives' tale said that the surest way to make a beard come in thick was to scrape it with a straight razor to "stimulate the follicles."

Not.

Every morning I rushed to the bathroom mirror and pored over my facial pores looking for anything, just one small sprig or microscopic frond that would indicate my manhood was on the way. Nothing.

Now, decades later, I am trying to appreciate the fact that Somebody Up There has a divine sense of irony, if not humour.

I finally have my coveted moustache—it's no Lanny McDonald but it's respectable.

Meanwhile, the top of my head is as bare as a Sylvania 60-watt bulb.

Good one, God.

Take Back the Night

Once upon another lifetime it was my honour to address the graduating students of a private school. When I'd exhausted my repertoire of pieties and platitudes the headmaster asked me if there was one piece of advice I could offer that would guarantee success in whatever they chose to do.

"Sure," I said. "I can tell you how a simple, easy, healthy, dirt-cheap alteration in your daily life will guarantee success. I can also guarantee that 99 percent of you will scoff and reject it the moment you hear it. Still game?"

They were.

So I gave it to them in three words: Get. Up. Early.

How early? Crack of dawn early, I told them. Get up early and work on your dream. Read, paint, sing, sketch, write, knit—whatever. Do just an hour or so early every day. They groaned and recoiled as if they'd been clubbed with baseball bats.

For once, I knew what I was talking about. Thirty-five years ago, when I was a husband, a new father and a holder of a full-time job it occurred to me that if I ever wanted to be anything more than the above, I needed to find some extra hours in my day.

It was summer, and I lived in a part of the country where the sun was already up and blazing at five in the morning. And so, after a few coughing, spluttering mornings, was I.

It's a grand time to get things done, the early morning. There is nothing on TV, no colleagues to drop by and chat. The rest of the family is asleep, the phone isn't likely to ring and it's way too early for Jehovah's Witnesses to be knocking at the door. Best of all the mind is fresh, rested and—after a jolt of java—frisky, even.

So I got up and wrote. Not absolutely every day (I took Sundays off and there was the odd morning compromised by flu or travel or a hangover that made it too painful). But almost every day—and I got more writing done in those precious one or two hours than I did in the rest of the week.

Productive? Well, fifteen books, five seasons' worth of TV scripts, uncountable TV and radio commentaries and a raft of speeches—all written in the early hours of the day. Oh, yes—and thirty-five years' worth of weekly newspaper columns. I'm not boasting about this, because it's no big deal. I didn't erect a cathedral or compose a symphony—all I did was get up early most mornings and sit down in front of a keyboard. It's like building a home or walking a hundred miles: it doesn't get done overnight, it gets done a brick or a step at a time.

Ah, but what about the hard part? What about rolling out of the sack at an hour when most folks are in deep sleep (and some are just rolling in from a night on the town)?

Yeah, there are compromises involved. An early riser doesn't get to close the bars or watch the *Late Late Show*. People who get up at dawn tend to go to bed earlier than most, which means your social life takes a bit of a hit. But there's nothing on television that you can't tape and watch at your convenience. And having one or two fewer beers with the gang won't do you any harm. *Au contraire.*

Best of all, you get to have some time to yourself to Get Something Done. Read your favourite author, complete a correspondence course, paint a watercolour, write those letters you've been putting off. Move your life along so that you're not merely putting in time.

There are other rewards, often unexpected. Some years after I gave my talk at the private school I got a phone call from someone whose name I didn't recognize. She was a film producer, working in Edmonton. She had also been a member of the student body in the school where I gave my talk.

"I just want to tell you," she said, "that I took your advice—about getting up early. It made all the difference in my career."

Yes!

Sung Any Good Songs Lately?

When you're thirty-five, something always happens to the music.

—GENE LEES

I first read that quote back when I was a teenager—which is way more tree rings than I care to count up. I remember thinking at the time: yeah, the man is right.

It explained why my old man couldn't get Elvis or Buddy Holly. When the strains of "Heartbreak Hotel" or "That'll Be the Day" would crackle out of our old Philco stand-up radio, my old man would throw down his newspaper and grouse, "What the hell is that? You call that singing? Can't even understand the words!"

Now, all these decades later whenever I hear a current top ten tune I find myself channelling my old man.

Are mushrooms growing in my ears or did the music change—as in, get stupider? At the risk of offending thousands I have to say that I find most modern popular music stupendously boring and appallingly mediocre. The vocalists sound like they're singing through keyholes; the instrumentalists sound like they're playing with boxing gloves on. Haven't these nimrods ever heard Ella or Aretha? A guitar solo by Chet Atkins or a trumpet riff by Wynton Marsalis?

Jimi Hendrix playing "The Star-Spangled Banner"—recorded live at Woodstock?

Aren't they embarrassed to pretend they're even in the same business?

How did popular music tumble from the dizzying glory of the Everly Brothers and the Temptations to the atonal squeaks and flatulent squawks that dominate the charts today?

Beats me. Beats Beck too.

That would be Bek David Campbell, a forty-something American singer, songwriter and multi-instrumentalist who prefers to be known as Beck. He's been around and on the charts for a good twenty years. Last year, Beck put out an album with a difference. Beck doesn't sing on this production, or play an instrument.

Nobody does.

Song Reader is not a CD or an LP or an iTunes download. *Song Reader* is a book of sheet music containing twenty original compositions along with a hundred pages of art. Beck's idea is to take listeners back in time, back to when people sang songs with and to each other.

"You watch an old film and see how people would dance together in the '20s, '30s and '40s," Beck told an Associated Press reporter. "It was something that was part of what brought people together. Playing music in the home is another aspect of that that's been lost."

Beck points out that nearly eight decades ago—in 1937—Bing Crosby recorded a song called "Sweet Leilani." Fifty-four million copies of the sheet music were sold. That means almost half the US population was trying to learn how to play and sing the song for themselves.

Well . . . yeah. When I was a kid, we didn't have a car or a TV but we had a piano in the parlour—as did most of the families I knew. And in our piano bench was a pair of castanets, a tambourine and a couple of dusty old harmonicas.

Mom and my older sister sang harmony, my other sister sang and played tambourine, while the old man chorded on the piano.

Me? I still play a fairly mean "Freight Train Blues" on the harmonica.

I know, I know . . . corny as hell.

On the other hand, I watched a family of four waiting for their dinner in a restaurant last night. They didn't talk. They didn't even look at each other. They were all texting, off in their separate corners of cyberspace.

I'll take corny.

A-Mushing We Shall Go—Not

I'm a double-edged, multi-tasking (some would call it obsessive-compulsive) kind of guy. I love doing two things at once because I hate wasting time. If I'm going to be stuck in a lineup at the bank, I take along a yo-yo. If I get caught in traffic jam I rat-a-tat the drum solo from "In-A-Gadda-Da-Vida" on the steering wheel with my thumbs. Even for short ferry rides I carry more gear than a Sherpa for Martha Stewart—food, magazines, my diary, a harmonica, even an inflatable pillow for naps.

When I heard about Canicross my first thought was: this is for me.

Canicross? The latest exercise craze. Apparently it began with some anonymous dogsledder in Lapland looking for a way to exercise his doggy cohorts in the summer, snowless months. What he or she came up with is essentially one-on-one dogsledding minus the sleigh.

Oh yeah—and instead of holding the reins, the human portion of the equation (formerly the sled driver) is lashed to the dog by a harness.

You're familiar with walking the dog? This is running the dog. Fido picks the trail and sets the pace. Your assignment is to keep up and stay vertical.

Oh, and in order to keep your hands free for balance (and to make it extra interesting) Fido is attached to your crotch.

Pretty much. The Canicross harness fits around your waist and loops about your upper thighs, terminating in a snap buckle in front of your . . . front. The buckle attaches to about six feet of leash, the other end of which clips to the dog's collar. All you have to say is "Go!" and you are officially Canicrossing.

Canicross is pretty green as sports go. Historians have traced it back to its Scandinavian origins in the early 1970s. Within a decade it had spread south to France, where the world's first Canicross meet was held in Paris in 1982. Since then it has blossomed, eventually hopping the Atlantic to take seed in Eastern Canada and parts of the US.

I know—you're asking yourself why would anyone willingly attach themselves to a dog and let it drag them through the bush.

Because in this hectic, stress-heavy world we're stuck with, where people fumble with their BlackBerrys even as the waiter is handing out menus; where parents text their offspring on the bus because it saves time—in our world, Canicross is the very essence of multi-tasking. It enables you to take care of two chores at once: your dog gets exercise and you get a serious cardiovascular workout.

How perfect is that? I've got a dog and I've got a gym membership. But there are not enough hours in my day to walk my dog AND toddle downtown to the gym. With Canicross, I don't have to.

I ordered the starter kit. It includes the human harness (they call it a hands-free belt)—for fifty-two dollars—and a pooch harness (they call it a Shorty Ripstop Sport Harness)—for thirty-four dollars. I donned the belt, attached a long leash to it and clipped the other end of the leash to my dog, Homer.

"Go!" I said.

I don't speak fluent canine and Homer is a critter of few barks, but I'm quite certain his response was the dog equivalent of "Huh?" Homer cocked his head, looked at me sideways, wagged his tail and sat down.

Homer (he is named after the doughnut-driven Homer of Springfield, not the Greek) is a bearded collie. He has never been a ball of fire, nor is he the Einstein of his breed—but he knows bedrock Stupid when he sees it. For the next hour we stumbled around the neighbourhood together, Homer sniffing, peeing, pausing briefly to scratch and then onward to sniff and pee and scratch some more.

Homer, I mean. I merely followed behind, a flunky biped, tethered to my dog by eighty-six bucks' worth of clearly superfluous yuppie gear.

Garrison Keillor famously said, "Dogs come when you call; cats take a message and get back to you." Mr. K. never met Homer, who is unmoved by the command "Come!" Nor does he respond to "Mush!"

Anybody want to buy a barely used Canicross starter kit?

Double Your Pleasure

I wouldn't tell just anybody this, but I suffer from Peanuts Envy.

"Peanuts," I hasten to add, was the sobriquet my Old Man bestowed upon my younger brother after he came home from the hospital wrapped in a blanket, red-faced, squally and looking very much like, well, an angry peanut.

I was twelve years old at the time, and unabashedly enthusiastic about having a younger bro. I looked forward to hours of road hockey and bike riding; of climbing trees and chasing pop flies. I anticipated the advantage of having an in-house fall guy to blame for my misdemeanours. I even imagined we might become a neighbourhood Force to Be Reckoned With.

"Uh-oh—here come the Black brothers." That had a nice ring to it.

Alas, a dozen years is a wide gap for kids to bond across. By the time he was in kindergarten, I was seventeen and discovering girls. When his voice went from falsetto to bass, I was hitchhiking around Europe.

We grew up apart but, oddly, came together in our adult lives. He met and married a West Coast island girl; I also made my way across the plains and over the Rockies to settle on the same island. The same street, in fact. We live a five-minute drive apart.

But it is a small island and my brother and I, despite the twelve years, look very much alike. Some have called us dead ringers. We get mistaken for each other. A lot. "Hi, Jim," a stranger calls out to me at the checkout counter. "How's it goin', Jim?" I'll hear from a passing motorist. I seldom correct them. It takes too long—and frankly, I'm flattered. Being mistaken for a twelve-years-younger version of yourself is a bit of an ego boost. But it's better than that. In addition to having inherited my outstanding good looks, ineffable charm and magnetic personality, my brother is an incorrigible flirt. He buys armfuls of roses on Valentine's Day and hands them out to every woman he meets. He hugs anyone who gives off a whiff of estrogen and treats her like a goddess.

He is, in short, a popular guy with the ladies. And if, every once in a while, some strange woman should mistake me for Jim and wrap herself around me in front of the town post office in a smothering embrace . . . well, where's the harm?

I figure if you're going to have a doppelgänger it's helpful to keep it in the family—although instances of mistaken identity are always fascinating.

True story: Once on a train to California, two blushing ladies approached a distinguished-looking silver-haired gentleman in the club car. "Have we the honour of speaking to Professor Einstein?" they gushed. "No, unfortunately not," said the stranger, "though I quite understand your mistake. He has the same unruly hair, but inside, my head is altogether different. However, he is an old friend of mine—would you like me to give you his autograph?" On the back of a train menu he wrote: "Albert Einstein, by way of his friend, Albert Schweitzer."

Oh, those Alberts. They all look alike.

FIFTY SHADES OF BLACK

PART TWO

Getting Along with the Neighbours

The Not-So-Friendly Skies

I observe but one cardinal rule as I am being prodded and scanned by sullen strangers in the meat processing and dignity-rendering plants our airports have become.

No joking.

No one-liners, Shaggy Dog stories, gags, puns or witty banter with the wand-wielding Gorgons at Security. If I see my old pal Jack in the lineup I may wave, semaphore, whistle, warble or tweet a greeting to him. What I will NOT do is bellow, "Hi, Jack!"

Generally speaking the Rent-a-Gropers who staff the security check-ins have limited imagination and absolutely zero sense of humour. I know that any behaviour I exhibit that separates me from the milling herd can lead to an exceedingly tiresome visit to, as Paul Simon called it, that Little Room.

And it's not getting better. Paul Chambers, a twenty-eight-year-old Englishman, was arrested and convicted for making a joke *while on his way* to the airport.

It happened like this. Chambers was en route to an airport in Yorkshire to take off for a winter vacation. A snowfall closed the airport. Chambers tweeted to his friends: "Crap! The airport's closed. They've got one week to get their s—t together; otherwise I'm blowing the airport sky high!"

A lame joke for sure—but Mr. Chambers did not send the message to the airport headquarters or to a newspaper reporter or a radio station hotline show—he sent it to his small circle of Twitter friends. His message was somehow intercepted and sent to the Yorkshire police. Chambers was duly arrested, charged and convicted of sending a "message of menacing character."

Mr. Chambers hired a lawyer and went to the High Court in London to have the conviction overturned. His defence? It wasn't a "message of menace"; it was a joke.

His lawyer opened the argument by quoting a line of poetry: "Come friendly bombs, and fall on Slough . . . " Surely the author of those words was at least as culpable as Mr. Chambers? Better hope not. The line comes from a poem by Britain's one-time poet laureate, John Betjeman. And it was meant as a joke.

Exhibit B: Some scurrilous advice from a chap named Shakespeare who wrote, "Let's kill all the lawyers." To which the Lord Chief Justice commented: "That was a good joke in 1600 and it is still a good joke now."

Mr. Chambers's lawyer added, "And it WAS a joke, my Lord."

Indeed. I'm happy to report that Mr. Chambers won his case, his conviction was quashed and it is once again okay to make jokes—even on Twitter. Even about airports.

And there are some splendid airport jokes. Such as the one involving a harried and self-important MP caught in a crowd at the MacDonald–Cartier airport in Ottawa. Once again, a snowstorm had hampered operations; flights were delayed and rerouted, passengers were milling around like herring and the lineups were long.

Nowhere longer than at the WestJet check-in booth where a harried ticket agent was doing her best to placate irate travellers. The MP barged through the line and bulled his way up to the desk, demanding a boarding pass. The ticket agent looked at him and said, "Sir, as you can see, there are many passengers ahead of you. We're doing our best to get everyone through just as quickly as possible. I'm afraid you'll have to get back in the line and wait your turn."

The MP went postal. He thumped the desk and roared, "DO YOU KNOW WHO I AM?"

Not missing a beat, the WestJet ticket agent picked up the public address microphone and announced to the entire airport, "Attention, please. We have a gentleman at the WestJet ticket counter who does not know who he is. Anyone who thinks they may know this man is asked at this time to please step forward and identify him. Thank you."

The crowd roared. The man snatched his wheeled suitcase and blustered off, tossing an obscene two-word curse over his shoulder.

The WestJet clerk picked up the microphone again and said sweetly, "I'm sorry, sir, but you'll have to get in line for that, too."

There Auto Be a Law

> *I think that the substitution of the internal combustion
> engine for the horse marked a very gloomy milestone in
> the progress of mankind.*
>
> —WINSTON CHURCHILL

I'm with the British Bulldog on this one. Oh, I rely on a gas guzzler
as much as the next person and I've had my nether parts kneaded
by enough saddles to know that going on horseback is no feasible
option—but that doesn't mean I'm in love with my car.

I believe future archaeologists will be dumbfounded when they see
how thoroughly we allowed automobiles to dominate our lives. They
transfigure our landscape, poison our air, dictate our habits, define
our habitations, suck our natural resources dry . . . and they kill us.
You think guns are dangerous? Gun fatalities account for less than
one hundred Canadian deaths a year. Fatal vehicle collisions claim
nearly thirty-five hundred lives annually. Put more graphically, guns
kill approximately one Canadian every six days; motor vehicles kill one
Canadian every four hours.

What they do to us socially is even more alarming. Marshall
McLuhan predicted that mass transportation such as subways and
trains was doomed in North America because, "a person's car is the
only place he can be alone and think."

That's what our vehicles do—they separate us. We don't walk or
stroll or—beautiful word—promenade anymore. Cars box us in. We
jump in our boxes and join streams of other boxes that take us to work

or to play or to shop—as often as not in boxy office towers, boxy rec centres or big box stores.

Happily, attitudes are changing. Many towns and villages—and even the tiny island I live on—are putting in pedestrian pathways and bike lanes for all those little trips that really don't require motorized assistance.

Cities too—and no city more comprehensively than Paris, France. There, the city fathers have okayed Vélib', a bike-sharing network that allows citizens to pick up a bicycle at one location, ride it to their destination and leave it there. They have also eliminated twenty-three thousand parking spots downtown, narrowed crosstown expressways and replaced pavement and parking lots with nearly ten acres worth of parks, floating gardens—even a flower market.

All of this in downtown Paris, which just a short time ago was characterized by honking horns, squealing tires and cursing drivers, all emanating from crawling daisy chains of cars and trucks courting terminal gridlock.

Has it changed the fabled City of Lights? *Bien sûr*. For one thing, you can actually see those lights now that the blue-black curtain of auto exhaust is dissipating. Car use in Paris has dropped a whopping 25 percent over the past decade. In the same time, bicycle use has doubled. One-half of all trips in Paris are now made on foot.

Vehicular diehards are aghast. They predict massive traffic jams and widespread chaos. The head of one pro-car lobby harrumphs, "We can no more eliminate cars from Paris roads than empty the Seine of water."

Fulminate away, monsieur. Other large urban jurisdictions are moving in the same direction as Paris. Across the channel, the city of London now levies a daily sixteen-dollar "congestion charge" on all private vehicles travelling downtown. Toronto, Montreal and Ottawa have already set up bike-sharing programs; Vancouver's working on it.

Personally, I think McLuhan was just a hair off the mark. Men don't love their cars because they allow us to be alone. That's what the bathroom is for. Men love their cars because it's the last place they can be in charge. Comedian Rita Rudner says car love is the reason most men are afraid to make a commitment to a woman.

"It's because we can't be steered."

Cambodia: Phoenix Rising

One of the more cynical rationalizations used by the US government for its use of drones to kill foreigners is the fact that there's a legal precedent. The official argument goes that it's okay to target enemies in their own countries because the US did the same thing to Cambodians during the Vietnam War.

True—but not something you'd think a country would want to brag about.

Back in the '60s and '70s during what became known as Henry Kissinger's Secret War, American bombers flew 230,000 separate sorties over Cambodia, dropping more than three million tons of bombs.

It was, as a US general said at the time, "the only war in town," since a temporary truce with Vietnam had been declared. It was also a bit like shooting fish in a barrel; the Cambodians had no air force, no anti-aircraft ordnance—no armed forces to speak of. They were mostly rice farmers. Their great crime was allowing the Viet Cong to use their country as a shortcut to South Vietnam.

Not that the Cambodians had much choice. They were as powerless against the Viet Cong as they were against the US bombers. The US military rationale was loopy at best; a bit like bombing Vancouver because it lies between Seattle and Alaska. Now the US is arguing that the thousands of innocent Cambodians who died as a result of the US pursuing North Vietnamese set a legal precedent, which makes it okay for the US to go after enemies in any neutral territory.

No one knows how many Cambodians died in the bombings, but estimates run as high as five hundred thousand. We do know that Cambodia was devastated, many of its towns reduced to rubble, the infrastructure shredded, its economy ruined.

Which made it easy for the monster known as Pol Pot and his Khmer Rouge to take over the country and utterly destroy what was left of it.

Pol Pot was Joseph Stalin on steroids. He practised social engineering with a sledgehammer and a meat cleaver. In four devastating years, Pol Pot oversaw the gutting and abandonment of all Cambodian urban centres. Organized religion was abolished, banks were closed, private property, markets and even money was eliminated. The Khmer Rouge tore down 95 percent of the country's Buddhist temples. Christians, Muslims, Chinese, ethnic Vietnamese and Thais were murdered on sight, as were government officials, professionals such as doctors or lawyers—indeed, all "intellectuals." Wearing eyeglasses was enough to get you branded an "intellectual."

Pol Pot's so-called Democratic Kampuchea was in fact a prison-camp state. One quarter of the population—about two and a half million people—were executed, died of disease or simply starved to death.

The best thing you can say about Pol Pot and his evil horde is that they only lasted for four years. He died under house arrest, probably a suicide, in 1998. Today, Cambodia has its old name back, a thriving tourist economy and best of all, a young and healthy growing population.

Especially young. Three-quarters of living Cambodians are too young to even remember Pol Pot.

But they'll have no trouble remembering the US bombings; it's a gift that keeps on giving. Those millions of tons of bombs that were dropped did not all detonate. Some experts estimate that 30 percent of them still lie in the jungle waiting to explode.

And they do, with deadly regularity. There are forty thousand amputees in Cambodia today, almost all of them victims of UXOs—unexploded ordnance. There will be many more amputees for decades to come.

"History," as Winston Churchill tartly observed, "is written by the victors."

How true. That's why no memorial on the face of the earth marks the passing of Pol Pot.

And Henry Kissinger, the architect of the Cambodian Secret War? Why, he won the Nobel Prize for Peace.

A Bellyful of Bad Guys

Not to be paranoid or anything, but don't be surprised if someday soon you're pulled aside by a couple of grim-looking dudes dressed in bad suits and dark glasses with curly wires coming out of their ears. As they shake you down they'll probably identify themselves as agents with the Disease Control Unit or Alien Surveillance Command or some such.

It's legit. They suspect you of harbouring and giving sustenance to alien life forms and you know what—they're right. You, my friend, are an enabler—a host. You are the front man for dangerous, possibly life-threatening creatures which are living and breeding, rent-free, at this very moment on your person.

You've heard of the Hole-in-the-Wall Gang? Well, this is the Hole-in-Your-Gut Gang. These nogoodniks are presently residing and conspiring in your belly button.

Interesting piece of business, the belly button—or umbilicus, as it's properly known. It's our only souvenir of the feeding tube—the umbilical cord—that sustained us all for the nine months we spent in our mommas' bellies.

Nobody goes through or gets out of this life without one—except I suppose Adam and Eve if you subscribe to the Garden of Eden miniseries. All Gaia's chillun—the placental ones anyway—got belly buttons, one to a customer. And for microscopic creepy-crawlies, what a perfectly swell condo-cum-cafeteria the average belly button is.

"Your belly button is a great place to grow up if you're a bacterium," says Dr. Tom Kottke of Regions Hospital in St. Paul, Minnesota. "It's warm, dark and moist—a perfect home."

And that's actually fortunate because not all bacteria are bad guys. Most of them, in fact, range from benign to positively healthy. Only a handful are what you'd call troublemakers, causing everything from leprosy, cholera and pneumonia all the way to ear and respiratory infections. Sounds ominous until you learn that researchers have identified more than twenty-three hundred types of human belly button bacteria so far—and most of them are as unthreatening as Anne of Green Gables at a strawberry social.

Are you an Innie or an Outie? If it's the latter, chances are the Men in Black will let you off with a stern warning. People with protruding belly buttons don't offer as hospitable digs for bacteria to thrive on. The odds are, however, that you're an Innie—90 percent of humans are. And 100 percent of belly button bacteria like that just fine.

Belly button infections are not unheard of, but they're relatively easily avoided. Simple soap and water usually does the trick.

For more stubborn cases though, there's always the military option. Bring out the big guns, I say. Warships, if necessary. Luckily we can do this without unduly taxing the resources of the Canadian Navy. You can build your own warship at home. Just root around in the attic or closet and find that old hula hoop you never got rid of. Next, insert a series of thumbtacks into the hoop perimeter, each one pointing inwards. Finally, put that hoop around your waist, crank up your Chubby Checker eight-track and gyrate vigorously.

Hey, presto! Your very own navel destroyer.

You Wanna Bet?

Gambling is a tax on people who can't do math.

—ANON

I am driving through the pre-dawn murk of an early summer morning en route to Pearson International Airport, a couple of hours away. I'm on a gravel road, no traffic in sight save an obese raccoon that waddles grumpily off the shoulder and into the brush as I pass.

No other signs of life, but a glow looms up over the trees on my left. I get past the trees and . . .

What

The Hell

Is That?

A neon fortress is what it is, huge and totally alien here in the Ontario hinterland. A sign in front tells me I'm passing Casino Rama and that Dolly Parton will be performing next week. My wristwatch tells me it is 6:15 in the morning. And my eyes tell me that the Casino Rama parking lot is nearly full.

Full??? At dawn????

You betchum, Lone Ranger. Casino Rama is the largest First Nations casino in Canada. It is run by and for the Chippewa of Rama First Nation and it is a right little gold mine. The facility boasts a hotel, a five-thousand-seat entertainment centre, ten restaurants and two lounges, but mostly it boasts twenty-five hundred glittering slot machines and one hundred and ten gaming tables, all dedicated to separating gullible patrons from their money.

No shortage of either. Casino Rama perches on the geographical forehead of the Greater Toronto Area, close to flush urban centres like Barrie, Lindsay and Midland. Literally millions of potential customers live within a bus ride of Casino Rama. Not surprisingly, the owners run free shuttle buses pretty much around the clock.

It's a pattern that's repeating itself around North America. The Mdewakanton Sioux of northern Minnesota used to be an impoverished and hopeless band of American Indian survivors existing on government handouts. Now they have Mystic Lake Casino, proceeds from which have financed a community and fitness centre, a hotel and an RV park.

The tribe has done so well it's been able to hand out more than half a billion dollars in loans and outright grants to other tribes for economic development. They even made enough from the casino to donate fifteen million dollars to the University of Minnesota for scholarships and a new stadium.

The Sioux have also set aside money to return to their roots, restoring wetlands to promote waterfowl, fish and wild rice plantings. They've put in organic gardens and planted fruit trees. And they've started an apiary to harvest honey.

But their most lucrative honey-making beehive is the glitzy Mystic Lake Casino, which attracts thousands of customers (overwhelmingly white) each week to lay their money down and watch it disappear.

It's quite a turnaround. Just a few hundred years ago First Nations people of North America lived in all the abundance they could handle. Then came the white man who, by judicious application of whisky, guns, syphilis and lawyers, changed all that.

In 1626 some European sharpie showered a band of East Coast Indians with sixty Dutch guilders' worth of trinkets, beads and hatchets. The Indians had no concept of land ownership, but they accepted the gifts. Later, they learned they'd just sold Manhattan Island.

Chief Dan George put it more succinctly: "At first we had the land and the white man had the Bible. Now we have the Bible and the white man has the land."

The great irony is, First Nations people through agencies like

Mystic Lake Casino and Casino Rama are slowly buying their land back.

And they're using the White Man's money to do it.

Comox Women Rock!

A woman needs a man like a fish needs a bicycle.
—IRINA DUNN

A lot of rock fans are positive that the group U2 invented that phrase. Others will beat you over the head with a bicycle pump insisting that Gloria Steinem deserves the credit. Actually, it was an Australian writer by the name of Irina Dunn, but attribution doesn't really matter; it's the sentiment that counts. A woman needs a man like a fish needs a bicycle. A Victoria cop takes down her would-be murderer even after he all but hacks off half her hand and stabs her in the neck. "Ninety percent of my officers would have died in that attack," says police chief Jamie Graham. Not Constable Lane Douglas-Hunt. She's back on duty as I write.

A woman named Alexandra Morton leads the campaign to get Norwegian fish farms out of our coastal waters; a woman named Elizabeth May leads the campaign to keep an oil pipeline to China out of our mountains and rivers and valleys. Six of our provincial premiers are women. Lots of Canadian women in leadership roles these days; no fish or bicycles need apply.

Still it was instructive to take a drive up Vancouver Island to the Comox Valley to deliver a keynote speech to the CVWBN. This stands for Comox Valley Womens' Business Network, a group of more than seventy local women entrepreneurs representing every profession from real estate to investment counselling, as well as bookkeeping, graphics, advertising, public relations—you name it, they do it, and they get together once a month to network, have dinner together and listen to an after-dinner speaker such as, well, that bald guy from Salt Spring.

As an observer it was fascinating for me. I couldn't get over how vibrant and sizzly the evening was, compared to a lot of guy get-togethers I've sat through. The businesswomen of Comox Valley really meet when they meet. It happened to be International Women's Day when I was their guest, and every woman stood up and said a few words about why she was glad to be a woman. I can't imagine even suggesting such a departure at any of the male-dominated get-togethers I attend.

The question I keep getting since I came back is: "So if the Comox Valley Women's Business Network is so powerful, how come they asked a man to be their guest speaker?"

I think the answer's pretty obvious. They're beyond that petty gender crap. If somebody's got something to say, it really doesn't matter how they're wired.

When Golda Meir became prime minister of Israel, a reporter asked her how it felt to be a woman prime minister. Golda shrugged and said, "I don't know; I've never been a man prime minister."

A Walk on the Wild Side

A few words about traffic jams. First, understand that I come from a Gulf Island that has (I'm being generous here) four, maybe five thousand cars, trucks, bicycles, skateboards, unicycles and other wheeled means of conveyance, all told. I have just returned from Vietnam. From Ho Chi Minh City, a.k.a. Saigon, which according to my guidebook contains some four million motorbikes. Not counting cars, taxis, buses, rickshaws, trucks or tuk-tuks. Just . . . motorbikes. Four million.

A traffic jam on Salt Spring occurs whenever two good old boys travelling in pickups in opposite directions on the same road, espy one another and stop for a chat through their driver-side windows while the traffic on both sides backs up behind them. We islanders seldom honk at the good old boys. We know they'll be done soon enough and traffic will resume.

A traffic jam in Saigon? Can't tell you. Never saw one. Oh, it's curb-to-curb chrome and rubber, all right. An absolute river of motorbikes and scooters and tuk-tuks, but like a river, it keeps moving. And like a river, there are back eddies and side streams and rapids and the odd whirlpool. Can't go forward on your motorbike? No problem: go up on the sidewalk. Still can't go forward? No problem: do a U-ey and go back. One-way street? No problem.

Sounds like chaos, and on Salt Spring it surely would be. But in Saigon, as in a river, it works. In three weeks I saw more motorbikes and scooters than I could see in three lifetimes on Salt Spring, but I saw only two motorized mishaps—and even they weren't proper traffic accidents. A motor scooter fell over while the owner was parking it, and another guy had his brakes freeze as he was crossing, well, a sidewalk, but that's another story. Point is: no damage, no injuries.

Ah, you say, but what about pedestrians? What about trying to cross that river of chrome and steel? Well, that's where it actually helps to be from BC. Especially if you've ever crossed a salmon stream while the fish were running. If you have, you know that if you walk slowly and steadily, those salmon—those tens of thousands of obsessed, hormone-besotted salmon—will not run into you. Their fins will tickle you; you will feel the ripples of water as their tails lash by—but head-on and T-bone collisions will not occur.

Same with the rivers of traffic in Saigon. If a pedestrian walks slowly and steadily and most of all with intent, those tooting, revving motorbikes and scooters will magically part on your upstream side and rejoin on the downstream stretch without so much as brushing your Tilley trousers.

It should be a disaster, traffic in Saigon, indeed in much of Southeast Asia. Stop signs are ignored, traffic lights are merely a broad suggestion, vehicles travel in every direction at once. It would be total chaos if we tried it here at home, but there, somehow, it works.

Day after day, night and day, the streets of Saigon, gorged with people and vehicles, continue somehow to function. It's an Act of Faith, crossing a Saigon street. Which is another thing that can't hurt. I know I said three Hail Marys before I stepped off the curb in Saigon. And I'm not even Catholic.

Make Mine a Double-Double

There are many things in this world beyond my feeble ken—nuclear physics, Microsoft Word, women—but a daily and ongoing bafflement is the corner coffee shop. How does that work exactly?

By which I mean: how do those enterprises stay in business?

From an outsider's perspective, it's economic hara-kiri. You have proprietors paying a hefty rent to occupy a trendy, expensively refurbished space to sell heated beverages to, well, basically, a roomful of freeloaders.

Granted, the cafe owners get a nice return on the four or five bucks they charge for a mug of hot water and .000003 cents' worth of ground beans, but still . . .

Think of the customer turnover compared to, say, a hamburger joint. At the Burger King the customers are sliding through like Jeep chassis on a Chrysler assembly line. And at the coffee shop? Well, the lady at the first table—the one hunched over her iPad next to the chai latte that's so old it's sprouting lily pads—is working on chapter twenty of her doctoral thesis on the influence of Rumi on neo-Renaissance architecture. At table two, a homeless guy wearing Bose headphones is puzzling over the *New York Times* crossword. The rest of the clientele is reading, writing, snoozing, gazing into space or murmuring sweet nothings into adjacent earholes.

Hardly any of them are buying and nobody's moving. I'm no

economist, but that does not sound like an outstanding model of mercantile viability.

And speaking of unsound business practices, who's the marketing genius who came up with the idea of offering free Internet access in coffee shops? Brilliant! Now every geek with a laptop who's still living with his parents has a free downtown office (with a heated bathroom and complimentary serviettes) where he can go and play Grand Theft Auto until his fingers bleed.

It makes no sense. And yet there is an intersection in downtown Vancouver that features a Starbucks on the northeast corner, a Starbucks on the southwest corner, and two independent coffee shops on the other two corners! They all appear to be crowded and they've been in business for years.

So what do I know?

Well, I know that some coffee shops seem to be feeling the pinch on their bottom line. They're taking down the "Free Internet" signs and taping up the electrical outlets in an effort to uproot the laptop squatters. There's a café in Chicago that's even resorted to flat-out bribery. If a squatter voluntarily gives up a seat when the place is crowded, management will buy that squatter a drink on the house.

Which, presumably, said squatter will sip while standing outside on the sidewalk, looking in.

Not every customer who goes to a coffee shop is a space hog, of course. A lot of customers line up and get their orders to take out—which again would make sound, efficient business sense if the customers were ordering a double cheeseburger with a side of fries to go.

They are not. They are ordering concoctions such as a half-skinny, half-chai, iced Frappuccino with whipped cream and a spritz of hazelnut syrup and an organically grown cinnamon stick on the side. Or possibly a demitasse of Ethiopian high-mountain dark roast pour-over with a decaf espresso shot and a lemon slice.

It's ironic. Coffee shops have been around since Shakespeare's time. They are the social equivalents of watering holes on the Serengeti—great places to meet with friends, catch up on the latest gossip.

The only problem: it's getting harder and harder to find anyone whose nose isn't buried in an iPad or—radical thought—to find a place where you can just get a cup of coffee.

Of course there's always the Canadian solution.

No upholstered chairs, no baristas at the bar, no po-mo computer graphics on the wall. Just fluorescent lights, Formica tables . . . and a queue that moves like Jeep chassis on a Chrysler assembly line.

Timmy Ho's. Make mine a double-double.

To go.

Of Beavers and Bullets

Know what I like best about Canada's national symbol, the beaver? It's not imperial. Not for us the American eagle with its razor talons, the British bulldog with its gobful of teeth or the ballsy Gallic rooster that struts symbolically for France.

Canadians chose a docile rodent with buckteeth, a potbelly and a tail that looks like it was run over by a Zamboni. We could have opted for a ferocious wolf, a majestic moose, a mighty bison or a fearsome polar bear.

We went with the flabby furball that wouldn't harm a black fly.

Maybe that set the pattern for our provincial emblems because they're pretty bland and inoffensive too. British Columbia has the Steller's jay; Newfoundland and Labrador went for the Atlantic puffin. For Ontario it's the common loon (perfect—what with having Ottawa and all) and New Brunswick stands behind the mighty black-capped chickadee.

I'm not sneering about this. I think it's positively endearing that Canadians chose non-threatening, peaceable symbols to represent their provinces. For our prickly cousins to the south, it's a little different. They go for *state guns*. Arizona has just proclaimed its official state firearm: the Colt single-action army revolver. It's the long-barrelled, six-cylinder shootin' iron favoured by Wyatt Earp and various other sanctified thugs of the American Wild West.

Arizona was late off the mark—the state of Utah has already declared its official state firearm: the Browning M1911, a semi-automatic .45 calibre handgun.

Is the Browning M1911 for hunting elk or target shooting? Nah. Its purpose is to kill people, period. It was developed by gun maker John Browning specifically for the US Army, which had put out tenders for a handgun powerful enough to drop an enemy soldier with a single shot.

I can see how the Army might lust after a powerful heater like the Browning M1911. It's more difficult to figure out why any state legislature feels it needs to honour an instrument the only purpose of which is homicide. You'd think that American politicians might be just a tad sensitive to the idea of venerating a weapon of semi–mass destruction after US congresswoman Gabrielle Giffords was shot along with eighteen other unarmed citizens in Tucson by a lunatic armed with— guess what? A semi-automatic handgun.

But then, Arizona has a different take on handguns—a different take on a lot of things—than most of us. It has a state reptile (the rattlesnake)—even a state tie (the bolo). And if you google "Arizona motorcycle seat" you will see an item that's very big among some bikers in the Grand Canyon state. It's a leather motorcycle saddle with a couple of extra features: along the back is a cartridge belt for bullets and on the flank is a holster for a long-barrelled revolver.

Just what I want to see thundering down the highway at me—a biker on a Harley with one hand on the throttle and the other thumbing back the hammer on his hog leg pistol.

Wouldn't raise an eyebrow in Arizona I guess. Former state senator Republican Lori Klein was asked in a 2011 interview if it was true that she carried a raspberry pink pistol in her purse.

"Aw, it's so cute," she enthused, as she pulled out a .380 Ruger and pointed it at the reporter's chest. The nervous reporter noted that the gun seemed to have no safety mechanism. Klein assured him that it was all right because she "didn't have a finger on the trigger."

Not every American politician takes a Dirty Harry attitude to guns. One of them once said this at a press conference: "With all the violence and murder and killings we've had in the United States, I think you'll agree that we must keep firearms from people who have no business with guns."

Sounds pretty reasonable to me, but what do I know—I'm a beaver boy, a Canadian. American politicians ignored the politician when he made that statement.

And that's a pity. His name was Robert F. Kennedy.

Of Diamonds and Medallions

Christmas, in all its weirdness, is coming.

Of course it's weird—flying reindeer? Trees in living rooms? Legions of non-union elves toiling above the Arctic Circle for room and board and one day off a year—you think that's normal?

And isn't it just a tad weird to look forward to a beard-o in a red suit slithering down the chimney in the middle of the night? To welcome a break and enter by a guy whose entire vocabulary consists of three "hos"? We Canucks are pretty happy-go-lucky about it. The Dutch? Not so much.

Dutch folklore features an Old Testament Santa, more Mafia don than jolly saint. In the Netherlands Sinterklaas rewards good kids with candy. Bad kids? Fuggedaboutit. They get a lump of coal.

Personally, I'd go for the lump of coal. I don't have much of a sweet tooth, for starters. Besides, it's been a long time since I held an actual chunk of anthracite. When I was a kid our cellar was half-full of the stuff every winter. I wasn't that enamoured of coal then because I had to shovel it into buckets and hump them upstairs to the fireplace.

So I can empathize with rebellious Dutch kids. Back when coal was the common source of domestic heat, getting a present of a chunk of the stuff was a bit like being slapped with a wet haddock.

Times change. Why, just last month a chunk of coal about the size of your ear sold at Sotheby's auction house in Geneva, Switzerland.

For a little over twelve million dollars.

True, it was a rather special lump of coal—found in a mine in South Africa last year and lovingly cut and polished by the finest craftsmen in New York. And they don't call it a lump of coal. They call it the Sun-Drop—the world's largest pear-shaped yellow diamond. (The buyer remains anonymous but I like to imagine he's some faceless, filthy rich Goldman-Sachs junk bond trader who parlayed some of his bailout money into a rock that he hopes will help him Get Lucky tonight.)

It's no secret that expensive things come in small packages, but usually those small things are intrinsically valuable, like the Sun-Drop diamond, a gold nugget or a baggie of Colombian marching powder.

But tin? Whoever heard of paying a million dollars for a piece of tin?

New York cabbies, that's who. One million dollars is the going price for the medallion that must, by law, be affixed to the hood of every legal Yellow Cab in New York City. What's more, it's a bargain.

It would have been smarter to pick one up back in 1937 when they first came out. The medallions sold for ten bucks a pop then. In the last three decades the price of a New York City cab medallion has soared by a gobsmacking 1,900 percent, making it more profitable than gold or oil.

The reason? Same as diamonds: scarcity. There are just over fourteen thousand medallions in circulation, a number that's hardly changed in seventy-five years. The NYC Taxi & Limousine Commission prefers to keep the medallions rare and treasured. So treasured that there's a company called Medallion Financial Corporation that exists solely to provide loans to cabbies who want to purchase their own medallion.

And how does a guy, earning a hack's wages, manage to do that? Simple, according to Andrew Murstein, president of Medallion Financial.

"A guy comes to this country, drives a cab six days a week, twelve hours a day, after three years, takes his whole life savings and puts it down to buy a medallion," Murstein said. "This is a way for him to get a piece of the American dream."

Sounds more like a nightmare to me, but then so does living in New York City. My pal Eddie says I'm a wuss and I've got it all wrong. He used to drive cab in the Big Apple. "People say New Yorkers can't get along," says Eddie. "Not true. Once I saw two New Yorkers—complete strangers—sharing a cab. One guy took the tires; the other guy took the radio."

Underground with the Viet Cong

I have no trouble accepting the premise that War Is Hell. I've never fought in one and impending geezerhood pretty much ensures I'll never have to. I thank my lucky stars for that.

But if the fickle Fates decide otherwise and the future finds me outfitted in helmet, army boots and twenty kilos' worth of combat kit on my back I have just one small request to make.

If I have to fight in a war, please don't make me fight it underground.

My recent trip to Southeast Asia included a visit to the Cu Chi district of Vietnam, a swath of lush jungle about fifty kilometres northwest of Ho Chi Minh City. Well, it's lush jungle now, but forty or fifty years ago it was a blasted and cratered moonscape of mud and shredded timber where nothing moved or grew.

That would be a direct result of the five hundred thousand tons of explosives US bombers had dropped on the area. They were trying to root out the Viet Cong who used the Cu Chi district as a military stronghold. All those bombs didn't make much difference because the Viet Cong were underground in an incredible network of tunnels that ran for 150 miles over a 100-square-mile area. But they weren't merely tunnels. The VC had constructed a maze, a complex—a virtual city that was three storeys deep in places. It incorporated sleeping quarters, meeting rooms, a command post, weapons storage, kitchens, emergency ORs—even weapons factories.

Actually, "factory" is gilding the lotus somewhat. A "factory" consisted of a few guys in black pyjamas hunkered down in the dark hammering and hacksawing chunks of bombshell debris.

As it happens, the soil in the Cu Chi area readily lends itself to the construction of tunnels. It's a mixture of clay, sand and rock that, on exposure to air, hardens like cement.

US forces weren't entirely unaware of the presence of the tunnels but they had no clue how extensive they were, and they weren't likely to find out by exploring them. The tunnels were low and narrow, built to accommodate the smaller bodies of Vietnamese, not a GI's strapping bulk. Then, too, the prospect of shimmying into a black void infested with poisonous spiders, venomous snakes, rats AND armed enemy soldiers, all in stifling jungle heat, can't have held much appeal. Accordingly, troops finding a concealed tunnel entrance usually elected to pump in poison gas or toss in a few grenades, fill in the entrance and move on.

So what was it like for the Viet Cong who lived in and fought out of the Cu Chi tunnels? Not good. Aside from being carpet-bombed almost daily, they suffered from a variety of pestilences. A captured Viet Cong document indicated that at any given time more than half the underground troops were stricken with malaria and that "one hundred percent had intestinal parasites of significance." Human beings aren't designed to live in tunnels. The air was bad, the diet was pathetic and the denizens had to learn to live in a permanent hunch in pretty much perpetual darkness. Viet Cong who didn't die outright suffered from severe vitamin deficiency that left them with enlarged heads, weak eyes, bad hearts, swollen feet and severe respiratory infections.

Sixteen thousand Viet Cong fought out of the Cu Chi tunnels during what they call "the American War." Twelve thousand of them lie buried in graves that carpet the outskirts of the tunnels.

Do the math. Three-quarters of the troops fighting for Ho Chi Minh in the Cu Chi tunnels died there. Clearly the whole tunnel offensive was a devastating defeat for the North Vietnamese forces.

And yet . . .

The official name of the nearest city is Ho Chi Minh City, not Saigon. It was changed in spirit the day a Viet Cong commando squad briefly but humiliatingly took over the US Embassy in Saigon during the Tet Offensive of 1968. Those Viet Cong operated out of the tunnels at Cu Chi.

The war is over and, incredibly, Western tourists are warmly welcomed in Vietnam. We can even tour short sections of the tunnels at Cu Chi—sections that have been purposely enlarged to accommodate our Western bodies. Even at that it's a cramped and uncomfortable experience—unimaginable as a way of life.

As one sweaty, wide-eyed Canadian tourist said, emerging into the sunlight from the Cu Chi tunnels, "No wonder they won."

Armed and Out to Lunch

What do you do when you realize the guy who lives next to you is nuts?

I don't mean "eccentric" or "dippy." I mean stark staring, bring-the-butterfly-nets nuts.

I thought about having him arrested, but I think he's got more pull with the cops than I have. Besides, he's pretty big—and he has a mean streak that stretches from here to Baghdad. I'm not talking about my personal next-door neighbour—he's fine (besides I've still got his lawnmower). No, I'm talking about OUR neighbour—the US of A.

Why do I think America's nuts? Let me count the ways. Let's start with the cartoon characters the Republican Party offered for presidential consideration last time around. Let's see . . . there was Newt the crook and Michele the loony; Cain the serial stickman and Rick Santorum, whom even the atrocious Ron Paul called "atrocious." At the bottom of the barrel they found a corporation called MITT, hooked it up to Lyin' Ryan and that's the ticket they ultimately went with.

But when you see how some other American elected officials turned out, maybe R&R Inc. wasn't such a nutty combo. Consider Judge Tom Head of Lubbock County, Texas. During the run-up to the election, the judge warned in a TV interview that if Republicans lost, the US would be invaded by United Nations troops. If Obama got the nod, Judge Head solemnly informed the TV audience, he would "hand over sovereignty of the US to the UN" and send in "UN troops with the little blue beanies."

Let me repeat: this is a judge speaking. He is a representative who was (presumably) democratically selected and elected as the candidate most suitable to interpret the laws of the country.

It isn't just Texas either. Lawmakers in Virginia recently wrestled with the problem of rising sea levels. Scientists have confirmed that those levels along the Virginia coastline have already risen a foot and are still rising. Grudgingly the lawmakers voted to fund a study of the problem—but only if all mention of "climate change" and "sea-level rise" was stricken from the bill. Reason? Because, said a spokesman for the Republican majority, "'sea-level rise' is a left-wing term."

Unfortunately, American nuttiness doesn't restrict itself to legislative bodies. It begins in the schools. A student by the name of Hunter Spanjer recently ran afoul of school authorities in Grand Island, Nebraska.

The boy is not your typical school delinquent; Hunter is four years old and deaf. Like most deaf people who use sign language, Hunter has a "nickname" gesture that he uses to identify himself. He points his index and middle finger together while he balls up his thumb and other fingers behind it. When Hunter introduces himself, he holds out his hand in this configuration and shakes it once or twice. That's how he says hello and it's kind of cute. Like a toy pistol. Hunter—get it?

Grand Island school officials got it. They ordered Hunter to cease and desist using the gesture because Grand Island Public Schools has a zero tolerance policy against "any instrument . . . that looks like a weapon."

Including a chubby pink fist attached to a four-year-old deaf kid.

Meanwhile, at the Republican National Convention in Tampa, Florida, officials banned water pistols, sticks, knives, even pieces of string—presumably because they might be construed as weapons.

But concealed pistols and automatic handguns? No problem, bring 'em on. Florida gun laws prohibit any local restriction on the carrying of guns.

In 2010, 170 Canadians died by guns, which is grisly enough. The number of Americans killed by guns in the same period: 8,775.

Bad enough when your next-door neighbour is nuts.

Even worse when he's armed.

Of Canaries and Chickens

You know the metaphor about the canary in the coal mine? Well into the twentieth century, underground miners carried caged canaries into mine shafts, where they kept one eye on the birds as they went about their work. When the canary fell off its perch, the miners downed tools and scrambled for the exit. Canaries are ultra-sensitive to toxic gases. If a canary had trouble breathing it indicated a carbon monoxide buildup that could eventually kill the miners.

Now, suppose you lived in New York City and on the morning of January 22, 2013, you decided to put your caged canary in front of an open window for a spot of fresh air. The bird would probably fluff up its feathers against the chill but it wouldn't croak. The Air Quality Index in New York on that date was a (relatively) healthy 19.

If, however, you lived in Beijing on January 22, 2013, and you plunked your caged canary in front of an open window . . .

Well, only a fool would have opened a window in Beijing on January 22, 2013. And if you did you'd be shopping for a new canary rather soon. The Air Quality Index for Beijing on that date read a staggering 755.

Let me repeat those figures. New York 19; Beijing 755.

How bad is air pollution when it hits 755? We don't have adjectives to describe it. Officially, China deems any reading above 300 as "hazardous." The World Health Organization judges a reading of 500 to be more than twenty times the level that's safe to breathe.

Nobody has a category for 755.

Here is what happens at that level: You cannot see across the street. Flights into and out of the city are cancelled due to zero visibility. Highways are closed for the same reason. Small animals are in distress; birds fall out of the sky.

And if you're a human you are, quite literally, on life support. Without an air purification system it is virtually impossible to breathe.

It didn't take an Al Gore visionary to see this coming. China has been exploding industrially, socially and commercially for decades. Canada has six cities with populations over a million; China has one hundred and sixty. More than twenty million live in Beijing. Worse, the city sits on a low, flat plain surrounded by mountains and thousands of factories. On windless days, Beijing is a massive cauldron of pollution.

Can China turn this around before it asphyxiates its citizenry? It's possible. China still enjoys the privileges of totalitarianism—which is to say the leaders can make things happen without going through the messy dance of democracy.

But you have to acknowledge a problem in order to deal with it, and historically despots are myopic when it comes to radical change.

One of the latest government responses came in the form of an official condemnation—not of the pollution outrage, but of reporters talking about the pollution outrage. A Chinese Foreign Ministry official blasted such reports as "not only confusing but also insulting."

The only insult in this sad story is the massive gang rape China is perpetrating on the planet. I don't know how canaries are faring in Chinese coal mines these days, but it's obvious the Chinese chickens are coming home to roost.

PART THREE

Human, Nature

Here's to Henny

A wife says to her husband, "You're always pushing me around and talking behind my back." He says, "What do you expect? You're in a wheelchair."

I was a stand-up comedian in a Vancouver nightclub for one night.

Scratch "one night"—about three minutes and twenty seconds. But it felt like it went on all night.

That's the one thing the audience and I agreed upon. They jeered and they hissed. They made unkind references to my lineage and addressed me in terms usually reserved for unmentionable parts of the anatomy.

What they did not do is laugh.

I have dog-paddled in shark-infested waters; I have let a live tarantula walk up my arm. I even mock-grappled with wrestler Gene Kiniski but I have never felt as desperate and lost as I did for those three minutes and twenty seconds in front of a hostile nightclub audience.

Not surprising. Studies show that the greatest fear for most people isn't falling off a cliff, being struck by lightning or getting mauled by a grizzly—it's standing up and speaking out before a roomful of strangers.

That applies to you and me, perhaps, but not to Henny Youngman.

The American (actually he was born in Liverpool, England) King of the One-Liners stood up in roomfuls of strangers virtually every day for over seventy years. He never took vacations or a weekend off. His audiences ranged from the *David Letterman* show to dinky wedding receptions in whatever hotel he happened to find himself. The film critic Roger Ebert remembered: "I once observed Henny Youngman taping a TV show in the old NBC studios. We got into an elevator together. It stopped at the second floor, a private club. A wedding was under way. Youngman got off the elevator, asked to meet the father of the bride and said, 'I'm Henny Youngman. I'll do ten minutes for a hundred dollars.'" He also did nightclubs (two hundred nights a year), the odd movie and a regular gig on *Rowan & Martin's Laugh-In*.

Youngman's humour was rapid-fire, machine-gun style. His act was only fifteen or twenty minutes long but he could cram a hundred different jokes into that time frame. Nobody ever complained about the length of Youngman's performances. Their sides were aching too much.

Youngman's wife, Sadie, was the butt of a lot of his jokes— including his trademark gag: "Take my wife—please!"

He had others:

"My wife said to me, 'For our anniversary I want to go somewhere I've never been before.' I said, 'Try the kitchen!'" Or: "Last night my wife said the weather outside wasn't fit for man or beast, so we both stayed home."

In fact, Youngman was nuts about Sadie and she returned the ardour. They were married for over six decades and toward the end when her health declined he had an intensive care unit built into her bedroom because she was terrified of hospitals.

Sadie died in 1987; Henny ploughed on for another decade, finally closing his remarkable one-man show in 1998 at the age of ninety-one.

Henny could spark laughs anytime, anywhere from anyone, but it never went to his head. For Henny it was a job. "I get on the plane. I go and do the job, grab the money and I come home and I keep it clean. Those are my rules. Sinatra does the same thing, only he has a helicopter waiting. That's the difference."

"Keeping it clean" was a big deal for Henny. I met a young comedian who got to sit beside him on an airplane once. The kid asked Youngman for his secret. "I keep it clean!" thundered Youngman. "All these young punks with their sewer mouths and their gutter jokes— stupid! Sure they get laughs but they don't get asked back because they offend people who don't like bad language. Best advice I can give you, kid—KEEP IT CLEAN!"

Then without missing a beat, Youngman buttonholed the flight attendant and said: "Now where's my #%$ing scotch?"

Caution: Boobs on Display

Got milk? You bet we have. More than six billion men, women and children drink that familiar white liquid produced from the glands of mammals every day on this planet. We downed 720 million tonnes of the stuff last year and there's no sign that our thirst is slaked.

And—aside from for those who are lactose intolerant—that's a good thing. Human breast milk is tailor-made for tiny humans but milk products of all kinds are healthy and plentiful and we don't just rely on two-legged mammals for our supply. We've guzzled our fill of milk from cattle, sheep, goats, yaks, water buffalo—even horses, reindeer and camels.

As for how we get the milk from the gland to the customer, well, that's changed a lot over the years too. I can remember when milk came to our doors in milk wagons hauled by patient, shuffling teams of horses. The one-quart bottles clinked and clanked as the wagon rolled along. Each bottle had a cardboard stopper and a tulip-shaped flare at the top, which is where an enterprising brat, if he tiptoed out on the porch early in the morning, could find the cream. Mmmmmm.

The horses were eventually retired and the milk wagons morphed into milk trucks that performed the same function. Then some bean counter worked out that it would be more profitable to have the customers schlep to a store and pick up their own supply of milk. Adios, milk truck.

The containers changed as well. The quart glass bottles were retired in favour of clunky, rigid polyethylene jugs, which in turn were replaced by soft plastic bags. After that came plasticized cartons in various sizes from quarter-pint (sorry, I'm a geezer)—all the way up to a two-litre version. I think that's how milk is sold in Canada these days, although I haven't been down to the corner store for a while so there may be yet another incarnation.

I also haven't been to downtown Pittsburgh, and that's a pity, because there's a milk delivery revolution going on down there. It's a big old ice-cream van that's been renovated. Each working day it winds through the streets of Pittsburgh with a giant pink fibreglass breast on top—complete with a rosy nipple that blinks.

It's called the Milk Truck, natch. Its purpose: to make life a little easier for breastfeeding moms. Inside there's a cozy lounge where mothers can find nursing supplies, breast pumps and a welcoming, non-hostile atmosphere. The crew, decked out in saucy milkmaid costumes, also responds to distress calls from nursing mothers in need of some privacy to pump breast milk during the workday.

The Milk Truck was the inspiration of Jill Miller, a Pittsburgh conceptual artist who created the idea as a commentary on attitudes to breastfeeding in public, then discovered that the Milk Truck was filling a real need.

But not for everyone. Ms. Miller was astounded to find that a substantial portion of the public is actually offended by the sight of women nursing their babies.

"We think nobody cares," she told a reporter from (really) *Bust* magazine, "but some people—predominantly women—are for some reason fully enraged by the thought of a woman feeding her baby in public."

Call me a slavering pervert but I think the sight of a nursing mother and child is about as beautiful as life gets. Tim Hortons customers lining up for their double-doubles wearing pyjamas and hair curlers— THAT'S offensive. But I digress.

I'd love to see Pittsburgh's Milk Truck rumbling down my street sporting a fibreglass breast with its nipple winking away.

And for any passerby who took offence? It would just prove that the real boob wasn't on the truck.

Got Beavers? Leave 'Em to Cougars

Whaddya gonna do when a mob shows up? A gang of fat little furry critters, buckteeth, flat tail, who mind their own business, vegetarian, non-aggressive, whose biggest fault is constructing unsolicited hydro preservation projects, usually in the middle of nowhere?

Well, you can make them the symbol of your nation and put their portrait on the back of the nickel. Or you could hunt them almost to extinction and turn their furry pelts into a high-fashion haberdashery statement.

We Canucks did both to the beaver. First we chased it, with traps and guns and clubs, from the sandy shores of the St. Lawrence to the shell beaches of Haida Gwaii, then, noticing that in our quest for furs we had accidentally discovered a country, we honoured the beast responsible with a little long overdue respect.

Well, sort of. Actually what happened is, High Fashion, as is its fickle way, grew tired of beaver hats, leaving trappers no very good reason to keep killing them. So, before the last beaver was turned into a homburg, we stopped. And the beavers, left on their own, did the thing that they're second best at—making little beavers. After two or three centuries there are once again plenty of beaver from Canadian coast to coast, and that includes at the end of a hiking trail in Dunbabin Park on Salt Spring Island.

Which in a long-winded way brings me to my point: we've got beavers in Dunbabin Park and we don't know what to do about it.

Normally, the answer would be "why do anything?" Salt Spring's a live-and-let-live place and we've got plenty of trees . . . what's the problem? Well, the problem is these are uncommonly ambitious beavers. The park trees these beavers are chawing on are not trembling aspens and willowy poplars. They're chowing down on the trunks of giant cedars, some of them more than a metre in diameter.

They haven't felled any of the big trees yet, and Parks staff has draped the damaged trunks with narrow-gauge chicken wire to discourage further demolition, but a lot of people are upset at the prospect of a park being flooded and clear-cut by a work crew of non-tax-paying aliens operating without a permit.

Which is ironic, because a human work crew with all the requisite permits recently clear-cut a swatch of forest just outside the park boundary, including by my count, at least thirty mature cedar and fir, which still lie a-mouldering on what's left of the forest floor.

But THAT clear-cut is legal and above board—even if it did do ten times the damage that a beaver colony could ever do.

And of course, the beavers aren't the aliens—we are. But being polite and quintessentially Canadian beavers, they'd never be so rude as to point that out.

I remain hopeful. I know it will take at least six months for Salt Springers to agree on ANY course of action vis-à-vis the beavers. In the meantime another couple of unlicensed aliens are prowling our forests—a pair of mature cougars. Cougars don't pay taxes either, but unlike beaver, they're not vegetarian.

I think if we just step back for once and leave it to Mother Nature . . . it might all work out.

To Beard or Not to Beard

There was a big photo of Thomas Mulcair on the cover of *Maclean's* magazine recently. STEPHEN HARPER HAS FINALLY MET HIS MATCH, the headline blared, in the magazine's trademark, understated, feces-disturbing way. The cover story mentions Mulcair's assets—a whip-sharp mind, a fast mouth and the disposition of a pit bull with ulcers. But what really separates the man from the guy who lives at 24 Sussex?

A beard.

The face fur separates Mulcair from just about every politician in Canada. It's an unspoken law, but a law nonetheless: if you're a man and you're running for office, your chops better be bare as a baby's backside. Voters, they say, won't trust a man with a beard.

Downright stupid, really. Jesus is always depicted with a beard. Abe Lincoln had a beard. Santa Claus has a beard.

Still, there have been a few bearded guys who did nothing to promote the brand. Taliban and al Qaeda lunatics wear beards. Saddam Hussein, when they hauled him out of his rat hole, sported a beard that resembled the south end of a northbound goat. Photographs of Karl Marx show a man who seems to be thrusting his face through a dehydrated hedge.

Marx looked like a choirboy compared to a seventeenth-century pirate named Edward Teach. A contemporary wrote that Teach was known by "that large Quantity of Hair, which, like a frightful Meteor, covered his whole Face, and frightened America more than any Comet that has appeared there in a long Time. This Beard was black, which he suffered to grow of an extravagant Length; as to Breadth, it came up to his Eyes; he was accustomed to twist it with Ribbons, in small Tails . . . and turn them about his Ears."

Teach was better known by his nickname, "Blackbeard."

Bearded bad guys are a relative rarity these days. Lots of popular figures—Brad Pitt, David Beckham, Johnny Depp—flirt with facial hair all the time. Even baby-faced Prince William grows a beard now and again—and looks much better for it.

Nevertheless beardophobia still thrives. Our armed forces take a dim view of any recruit who shows up with a beard. How to Get a Job manuals and Miss Manners columns invariably recommend a "clean-shaven" look.

Even my sainted mother went to her reward tsk-tsking and tut-tutting about her wayward eldest son and his unshorn mug. "No woman is ever going to want to kiss that," she told me. Often.

Sorry Mom, but you were dead wrong on this one. As soon as I could, I grew myself a beard. Not for me the Vandyke, the French Fork or the Mutton Chops. Fie on the Chinstrap, the Soul Patch or the Goatee. I grew myself the Full Monty—jungle foliage from sideburns to Adam's apple.

And it paid off. I knew my beard was a turn-on the first day I showed up for my bartending job that helped pay my college bills.

Women dig beards. I still remember that beautiful blonde coming out of the washroom and undulating up to the bar where I was washing glasses. "Are you the manager?" she cooed, sitting down and pointing her cleavage at me. I stammered that I wasn't. She reached a hand across the bar and caressed my beard. "Oh, that's too bad," she pouted, and brought her other hand up and ran it alongside my chin, twisting my whiskers gently into ringlets, "because I'd like to leave him a message."

"I could give him a message," I squeaked. I could hardly talk by now. She was practically giving me a full facial massage.

"Good," she purred. "Tell him the ladies' room is out of toilet paper and hand towels."

Canadian Heroes, Subspecies: Unsung

F. Scott Fitzgerald once wrote, "Show me a hero and I will write you a tragedy." Well, I don't know about that, but I'll show you a hero. A family of them in fact: the Murakami family of Salt Spring Island.

There are three of them left, Richard, Rose and Violet, all siblings. They are all getting up there, in their seventies and eighties, but they've lived on Salt Spring Island all their lives. Well, that's not quite true. They spent some time inland back during the war.

The Murakamis are Canadians of Japanese descent. A 1941 census counted seventy-seven Japanese Canadians living on the island—a substantial portion of the entire population back then. Twelve months later there were exactly no Japanese Canadians living on Salt Spring. They had all—farmers, fishermen, businessmen and their families—been rounded up like Holsteins and railroaded off to work camps in Alberta and the BC Interior. Their businesses, their farms, their livestock, their fishing boats and gear had been commandeered and then sold off to the white folks.

The Murakamis came back to Salt Spring Island after the war—the only Japanese Canadians to do so—only to find that everything they'd owned was gone. But there's a word in Japanese—*ganbaru*—which means approximately "slug it out," "do your best," "don't give in." The Murakamis didn't. They started again from scratch and reseeded themselves on Salt Spring. Nearly seven decades after they were shipped away in cattle cars, the Murakamis thrive on Salt Spring. They still live together, Richard, Rose and Violet, in a spacious house overlooking their gardens and Richard's shop.

He runs Salt Spring's most famous auto repair business, employs a half dozen mechanics, most of whom are receiving their old age pension. They all answer to Richard, who pads around his hangar-style repair shop all day long, joking with customers, hauling his duct-taped cellphone out of his overalls to take calls and order parts and generally overseeing the task of keeping most of Salt Spring's beaters and clunkers on the road.

And Richard? He answers to his sister Rose, who controls the finances and presides over the Murakami home. Rose is hardly your typical farm girl. She is an author and a lecturer with a master's degree in nursing and she formerly served as chief nursing officer at the University of British Columbia Health Sciences Centre.

An amazing family, the Murakamis, about as close to royalty as Salt Spring will ever get. And are they revered and honoured like royalty? By most islanders, yes. But not by all. This ain't Disneyland, chum—it's Salt Spring. I've heard one islander claim that what happened to the Murakamis during the war wasn't anybody's fault, it was just . . . the times.

So that made it okay to steal their homes and farms and fishing boats???

The Mounties still hassle Richard about cars parked across the road from his garage. And right now the Murakamis are looking at a court order to get rid of the derelict auto wrecks in his back field. Those junkers are there because Richard took them off the hands of owners who were done with them but didn't want to pay to have them hauled off the island.

Now some citizen (who naturally wishes to remain anonymous) has complained to authorities, and the Murakamis have one more legal headache to contend with.

My personal opinion? I think the Murakamis should be given a blank cheque, free room and board, a party once a month, the keys to the island and a lifetime supply of the beverage of their choice for what we've taken away from them and for what they've given back to us.

Which includes, by the way a prime chunk of land on which sit twenty-seven affordable housing units right in downtown Ganges. The Murakamis donated that prime land, gratis. They may be getting on, but they still remember what it feels like to be homeless.

Kilroy Wasn't There

He's been following me all my life.

Correction: I'VE been following HIM all my life.

He's beaten me to every significant place I've visited: national monuments, public washrooms, bulletin boards—even pages of books.

It's Kilroy I'm talking about. You know the guy? Leaves a cartoon drawing of himself—just two eyes and a big nose peeping over what looks like the top of a fence. Under that he prints his characteristic one-line calling card—KILROY WAS HERE.

The Kilroy trademark began appearing way back during World War II when American GIs took up the practice of scrawling Kilroy's inquisitive schnozz and tag line at battle sites in Germany, Italy—even on palm trees of engagement zones in the Pacific. It wasn't long before civilians got into the act. The slogan began showing up all around the world. You could find KILROY WAS HERE graffiti on the Sphinx, the Arc de Triomphe, the Statue of Liberty—even atop Mount Everest. Legend has it that an Apollo astronaut even scrawled it in dust on the moon.

It's a fascinating illustration of how even a trivial, meaningless bit of pop culture fluff can, for no discernible reason, go viral and spread around the globe.

Except for one thing: KILROY WAS HERE is not a meaningless phrase. There really was a Kilroy and he really did come up with that famous slogan.

His full name was James Kilroy and he was an inspector at the Fore River Shipyard in Quincy, Massachusetts. One of his jobs was to keep track of the number of rivets shipyard workers installed every day. He would tally up the number and put a check mark beside the last rivet so that they wouldn't be counted twice. The workers—who got paid by the number of rivets they placed—quickly wised up and started erasing the check marks, fooling the next inspector into recounting the rivets and paying them extra. When James Kilroy wised up to the scam, he added his cartoon and the line KILROY WAS HERE to the check mark. End of accounting problem—and beginning of a world-wide phenomenon. The story goes that when Joseph Stalin emerged from the VIP washroom at the Big Three conference at Potsdam in 1945 the first question he had for his aide was, "Who is this Kilroy?" Reminds me of the Stan and Si.

"Stan and Si" is a sandwich. When I was younger and lived in Thunder Bay, Ontario, I frequently went into restaurants and ordered a Stan and Si—as did many others. It wasn't always printed on the menu, but the waitress inevitably knew what you meant—basically a hot roast beef sandwich with some extra trimmings.

A local newspaper editor explained to me that Stan and Si were two Thunder Bay railroad workers who liked to shoot a game of pool on their lunch hour. They didn't have time to sit down so they'd order their favourite sandwich and eat it while they played. Pretty soon their lunch became known as "the Stan and Si." It's still available at select Thunder Bay establishments, as far as I know.

Next time I'm in the Lakehead I plan to find out for sure. I'll hit the first restaurant I see and order a Stan and Si with a side of fries.

If they know what it is and bring me one, I'll scrawl KILROY WAS HERE on the menu.

In Vietnam, Don't Order the Mutt-on

I have just come back from Vietnam, where I have seen many amazing things, including Ho Chi Minh himself. What's left of Uncle Ho (his mummified corpse) reposes on display in a gargantuan, graceless mausoleum in the centre of Hanoi. I saw other amazing things in Vietnam—pagodas, sacred caves, water buffalo placidly plodding through rice paddies, sylphlike sampans, graceful as eyelashes, skimming the surface of canals and rivers . . .

But I think the most amazing thing I saw was motorbikes. Motorbikes are to the Vietnamese today what the automobile was to North Americans in the 1950s. Times ten.

In Saigon alone (nobody other than government flunkies call it Ho Chi Minh City) there are four million motorbikes. That is not a misprint. Four million. Virtually every Saigon family owns at least one. It functions as the family station wagon does for us. Again—times ten.

It is not uncommon to see a family of five on one motorbike, the youngest wedged between the handlebars, the rest hanging on any way they can. It is also not uncommon to see motorbikes carrying multiple bags of animal feed, freakishly high tiers of lumber, a refrigerator (I'm not making this up), twenty-foot stepladders, butchered hogs, mattresses, aluminum doors, toilet bowls . . .

And—Culture Shock 101—crates stuffed with live animals, including puppies.

Saw this myself from a bus outside Hue—a little Honda

putt-putting along, one rider, with a dozen wooden crates full of what looked like Akitas or huskies, weaned, maybe three months old, lashed down and teetering behind him.

And you just know they weren't heading for the Hanoi Obedience and Agility Dog Trials.

Unpalatable fact: Southeast Asians eat dog—or some of them do. It's an old tradition bound up with beliefs about the merits of dog meat as an energy booster and an aphrodisiac.

The natives are aware that canine entrees on the menu would make tourists nervous if not hysterical, so you don't see *escalope de poodle* or barbecued border collie advertised, but if you go to an obscure Thai or Vietnamese restaurant that caters to locals you might come across a dish called, ironically enough, *pad krapaw.*

That's, um, stir-fried dog meat with basil leaves.

Eating dog meat is, I'm delighted to report, a disappearing feature of Southeast Asian life. It's a cuisine phenomenon mostly restricted to working-class clientele. Kids in school are being taught that it's not cool to eat pets—and in any case it's relatively expensive, dogs being more rare than carp or chickens.

Did I try it? Get serious. I'm a bourgeois North American geezer. I'm so reactionary I seldom even buy sushi—unless I'm fishing and I run out of bait.

Besides, I knew if I indulged I would have to avoid eye contact forever with a bearded collie and a golden retriever/border collie cross back home.

Still, I didn't raise a fuss when I saw unfamiliar, possibly pooch-oriented entrees on the odd Southeast Asian menus. Wouldn't do for me as a Canadian to get too holier-than-thou over animal cruelty. I remember two other times when I saw cages of animals crammed together and stacked in tiers.

In one case the cages were stuffed with battery hens on a "factory farm" in Southern Ontario; the other time was a barnyard crammed with tiny, windowless plastic cubes on a farm near Vancouver. The cubes were the only home that veal calves, brusquely separated from their mamas, would ever know. Southeast Asians can't teach North Americans much about cruelty to animals.

Would You Read This, Please?

The test of good manners is to be able to put up pleasantly with bad ones.

—Wendell Wilkie

I'm worried about the increasing disappearance—and possible pending extinction—of two critical English language expressions.

Those expressions are: (a) Please and (b) Thank you.

Used to be common as song sparrows, those expressions. "Could you pass the potatoes, please?" "Yes, here you are." "Thank you."

I can still cast out as many pleases as I want, but I seldom hook a thank you. Instead I reel in "No worries," "Sure," "Cheers," "No problem," "You betcha," "Right" and occasionally "Have a good one."

Such expressions are hardly hostile, but they're also not quite as heartfelt or sincere as a simple thank you. There's an ironic aura of "no big deal" about them. They don't represent a connection between two people; it's more like a disconnection.

Lisa Gache, a consultant in Los Angeles, has noticed too. She says what used to be common courtesy in civil discourse is on the way out and being replaced by all things casual. "Casual conversation, casual dress and casual behavior have hijacked practically all areas of life," she says, "and I do not think it is doing anyone a service."

Wade Davis, the Canadian anthropologist, ethnobotanist, author and photographer, travels the world but when he's in North America, he says, it's never hard to tell whether he's north or south of the border. Just go in the nearest supermarket. In Canada, he says, you usually have eye contact with the cashier and a brief conversation, while in the US the transaction is totally impersonal. You could be dealing with a robot. Davis says it's a class thing. In Canada, the chances are very good that the cashier's kids and your kids go to the same school, play on the same soccer team and live in the same neighbourhood. Whereas in an American store you're often dealing with a bussed-in, part-time worker from a poorer neighbourhood, working for minimum wage and living in a whole different society. Why would she or he be friendly? Aside from a few bags of groceries on the checkout counter you two have almost nothing in common.

I notice a growing remoteness with the people I deal with in public here in Canada. My partner, who has a way of crystallizing my various melodramas, laughed when I mentioned the Public Chill.

"What do you expect—you're a geezer," she said. "That makes you invisible to anyone under twenty-five."

A retired scientist I know concurs. "We've noticed that the lack of acknowledgement and general politeness isn't confined to strangers," he writes. "Neighbours, friends and even spouses of our children seem to have a hard time giving thanks of any kind."

Maybe it is just a generational thing. If so, there are signs that some adults are getting a little tired of being treated like doormats. Tom Jordan of North Carolina, for instance, who discovered that his fifteen-year-old daughter, Hannah, was cursing her parents out on Facebook, telling the world they treated her "like a damn slave" because they expected her to do chores around the house.

Dad took the laptop out in the yard, set up a webcam, shot the laptop nine times with a gun and posted the video to YouTube for "all those kids who thought it was cool how rebellious you were."

Now that's an extreme (and extremely American) reaction to bad manners. I prefer the approach taken by the famous actress Ethel Barrymore, who once invited a young actress to a dinner party. Not only did the guest not appear, she didn't bother to let Barrymore know in advance, or to account for her absence afterward. Several days later the two women met unexpectedly.

"I think I was invited to your house for dinner last week," the young actress said lamely.

"Oh, yes," replied Barrymore brightly. "Did you come?"

Forever Moe

If you saw him lumbering across the green—baggy sweater, rumpled work pants, built like a refrigerator, red-faced under a thatch of unruly hair—you'd assume he was there to rake the sand traps.

You'd never guess you were looking at the best golfer in the world. Not my opinion—Vijay Singh's. Lee Trevino called him "a genius." Sam Snead said he was the best ball striker he'd ever seen. Tiger Woods said that only two golfers in history "owned their swings." One was Ben Hogan; the other was that farm kid from Kitchener, Ontario—what was his name? Oh, yeah—Norman. Moe Norman.

They called him Pipeline Moe because he could line a golf ball straight as a laser beam, shot after shot after shot. Ben Hogan wasn't buying. Hogan claimed that any golf shot that went straight was "an accident." One day he stood behind Moe as he pounded a ball arrow-straight down the fairway. "Accident," murmured Hogan. Moe teed off another one. "Accident," said Hogan. After six more drives Hogan shook his head and walked off, muttering, "Keep hitting those accidents, kid."

Moe Norman wasn't a golfing legend; he was a golfing god. A score of sixty is considered a perfect game, virtually unattainable. Moe carded three games of fifty-nine and four of sixty-one. Most golfers only dream of a hole-in-one. Moe had seventeen. He owned the course record at thirty different clubs. He held multiple championships from

Ontario, Manitoba, Saskatchewan and Alberta and the approbation of every knowledgeable golfer on the continent.

So how come the rest of us never heard of him?

Because Norman was paralyzingly shy. It's a wonder he ever worked up the nerve to swing a club in front of spectators; in most social situations, Moe couldn't string two words together. When he won the Canadian Golf Championship in 1955, officials couldn't find him to present the cup. Moe was hiding in the locker room.

No one knows why Moe was so profoundly uncomfortable in public, but that and his volcanic temper (snubbed by a PGA functionary for violating the dress code, Moe swore he would never play in the US again—and he didn't) consigned Moe to the sidelines of the pro golfing world. He played in exhibition matches, even played rounds "back to front"—driving with a putter, putting with his driver—and still made par. He drove himself from tournament to tournament in his dusty old Cadillac (which he slept in, usually), subsisting on junk food and winning enough to keep him on the circuit.

He dominated the Canadian golf scene in the 1950s but he shunned the Bigs, perhaps afraid of being embarrassed again. Lee Trevino: "I think if someone had just taken Moe under their wing and said, 'Look, we're going to play here, don't be afraid'—there's no telling what Moe Norman could have won."

He mesmerized onlookers, including the president of Titleist Corporation, who was so impressed he offered a lifetime contract that paid Moe five thousand dollars a month. Just to play golf.

It was generous, but it was late. Moe was sixty-six by then, and past his prime. Nine years later he was dead, of congestive heart failure.

But the anecdotes live on. Such as the time he and Sam Snead were playing a fairway intersected by a creek 240 yards away. Snead warned Moe he couldn't clear the creek with a driver. "Not trying to," said Moe. "I'm playing for the bridge." Snead's shot landed on the near side of the creek; Moe's landed on the bridge, then dribbled across to the other side.

Ho-hum. Just another Moe Norman accident.

Just a Card to Say: Way to Go!

A word or two on behalf of the postcard.

I know—they're hopelessly old-fashioned. Went out with hoop skirts and penny-farthing bicycles. Imagine sitting down to write a card to someone. First, you have to think of something to say, then you have to look up their mailing address after which you have to cough up—what is it, close to a buck now?—for a stamp. Finally, you have to find yourself a post box (good luck with that) to drop the card in.

Oh yes—and brush up your penmanship skills so you don't come off looking like a drunk or a chimp playing with a ballpoint.

Put yourself through all that when you've got the option of hauling out your cell and tweeting them in a nanosecond? Ridiculous.

And yet . . . there's something about a postcard that no BlackBerry, iPhone or Android device can match. A postcard is from me to you—not from one device to another. And the fact that so much time passes between thinking of writing it and popping it in the mail means consideration is involved. You have time to think about what you're saying. It's not just tap it out and press "SEND."

There is one other, ah, factor that makes me personally fond of sending postcards.

I happen to have several thousand of them in my attic. Unused. They are blank on one side; the other side shows a photo of me under the banner "BASIC BLACK." I used to host a weekly radio show on CBC by that name. I retired ten years ago and while cleaning out my office I noticed three boxes of unsullied *Basic Black* postcards stacked by the garbage can. I asked the janitor what was happening with them. "They'll be shredded, I guess."

A high, keening wail filled the halls of the CBC. It was the wraith of my ancient departed Scottish grandmother wailing, "Och, aye, ye'll no be wastin' those, laddie."And I didn't. I took those boxes home and for the past ten years I've been scribbling on their backsides and sending them out to whoever tickled my fancy.

A friend asked me if I didn't feel a little weird, sending out postcards advertising a radio show that's been off the air for a decade. Not at all, I said. I look on them as tiny retro gifts from an age gone by that I send to people I admire. What's more, postcards impose a necessary brevity that is almost poetic. The reduced message area means you really have to think about what you write—no room for discursive ramblings about weather, your wonky knee or the hapless Blue Jays.

As for whom to send a card to—for that I take the advice of a writer named James Mangan, who says those postcards and letters matter a great deal—even if all they say is "Attaboy!"

"Write to the author whose story gave you a delightful half-hour last night," says Mangan. "Write to the cartoonist whose strip you devoured this morning; to the teacher who inspired you twenty years ago; to the doctor who saved your baby's life; to your old employer to show him there was something more between you than a paycheque."

You get the picture. There are dozens—probably hundreds—of people you've fantasized about patting on the back and saying "Well done" to. A phone call is a bit over the top and a tweet or an email would just be, well, a tweet or an email.

Perhaps it's an Air Canada flight attendant who found your missing wallet or a Paralympics wheelchair racer who made your heartstrings twang. A grocery clerk who smiled when you needed it badly; perhaps a politician who did the right, instead of the expedient, thing. The world is full of people who behave better than they absolutely have to. Won't you send at least one of them a note or postcard to tell them so?

Attaboy!

Sally Armstrong: Hero

When I retired from hosting *Basic Black* in 1992 it meant, among other things, giving up my weekly commute to Vancouver. At my retirement party a producer sidled up to me and said, "Are you sure you can handle living full time on Salt Spring? I mean, I know it's peaceful and all, but man, it's the boonies! You'll go stir-crazy."

Well, I'm ten years in and I wish I could sidle up to that producer and say, "Were you drunk?" I'm as busy as I ever was when I slogged off to Vancouver every week. The only things no longer in my life are police sirens, panhandlers and getting stuck in the George Massey Tunnel in rush hour.

Okay, and a weekly paycheque. That's missing too. But as for outside stimulation, that's not a big problem on Salt Spring. In the last month I've been to talks by Robert Bateman and Wade Douglas; I've seen the movies *The Artist* and *The Hunger Games*; spent an evening listening to world-renowned blues harmonica virtuoso Carlos del Junco . . .

Oh yeah, and I got to hear Sally Armstrong, too. She spoke at the Salt Spring Legion and she is a powerhouse. I first met her a million years ago when she was editor of *Homemakers* magazine and I was a freelancer trying to sell her a story about a brothel in Thunder Bay.

That story didn't pan out, because of a lack of enthusiasm. Not on Sally's part; she was gung-ho but I kind of lost interest when I discovered that the proprietors of the brothel had strong-ish Montreal Mafia connections.

But that, as Sally would probably say, is another story. She uses that phrase a lot as she segues from one chapter to another of her turbulent life. She's been an editor and a columnist and a reporter and a documentary filmmaker. She's hit most of the world's hellholes: Rwanda, Somalia, Bosnia, Bangladesh. She's spent much of the past fifteen years in that hellhole of hellholes—Afghanistan. She specializes in investigating zones of conflict—specifically, the plight of girls and women trapped there. She's not doing it as a sightseer or a thrill-seeker. Sally Armstrong wants to change things. And she thinks that mobilizing the women is the way to do it.

Hard to argue. Males have been in charge of those hellholes since forever, and look at the mess they've made. And contrary to the tone we detect on the news, Sally Armstrong is optimistic about Afghanistan's future—albeit guardedly. She talks about the actions of one group called Canadian Women for Women in Afghanistan. It's headquartered in Calgary but has volunteer chapters across the country. They threw a series of potluck suppers, "that most Canadian of institutions," as Armstrong calls them. They raised enough money to put *fifty thousand* Afghan girls in schools. It doesn't take billions. An Afghan teacher earns about $750 a year. And when you're in a country with an illiteracy rate of 85 percent, the only way out is up.

More importantly, women in Afghanistan are taking their first shaky steps in support of women in Afghanistan. Armstrong told the story of Noorjahan Akbar, a student who started a group in Kabul called Young Women for Change. They collect books, set up libraries, arrange lectures. She's just twenty-one, but 65 percent of Afghanis are under the age of twenty-five.

They've only known bombs and blood and chaos and corruption but they have access to iPhones and the Internet and they want something different. With agents like Sally Armstrong and Noorjahan Akbar spreading the word, in venues as various as Kabul markets and the Salt Spring Legion . . . they just might have a shot at it.

Cuts Like a Knife

I once saw the oldest knife in the world—well, the oldest one we've found, so far. It was in a British museum and came all the way from a gorge in Africa. It was just a chunk of volcanic rock chipped with another stone until it was roughly triangular, rounded at the top for a handhold, tapering in two sharp edges to a dagger point. Custom fabrication by some nameless prehistoric toolmaker a million and a half years ago. Didn't look like much, but in terms of human evolution it was as important as fire, the wheel and $E = MC^2$. That knife was our equalizer. We didn't have teeth like a shark or talons like a lion or speed like a cheetah or muscles like a bear. But we had a knife, and before long (in evolutionary terms) mankind would have spears and arrows and, in another blink of the evolutionary eye, hunting rifles and fish-finding radar.

Knives continued to evolve, too. Today we have penknives, jack-knives, Barlow knives and Bowie knives. On the sinister side we have bayonets, stilettos and switchblades; on the utilitarian side we have machetes, pruning knives, paring knives and potato peelers.

Knives aren't the only things that have evolved. So have knife makers. On my island, Salt Spring, lives a man who is a natural descendant of that Stone Age African craftsman who smashed rocks together to make an edge sharp enough to cut flesh nearly two million years ago. The descendant's name is Seth Cosmo Burton and he is a maker of knives. Cosmo knives, he calls them. He often uses rock too, but only for the handles of his creations and only the finest of rock—jade, lapis lazuli, marble, sodalite and Salt Spring flowerstone.

As for the blades, they're in a class by themselves. Burton started out making steel blades the conventional way, but—well, he evolved. Now he uses a process called crucible particle metallurgy to smelt his metal on his own forge. It gives a sharper, harder, purer edge to the steel.

Burton's made all kinds of knives, from pocket to hunting, but he seems to be turning to chef's cutlery now and chefs seem to appreciate his attention. Chef Bruce Wood says his Cosmo chef's knife is quite simply the nicest one he's ever used. Anthony Sedlak, who hosted a show on The Food Network, said Cosmo knives are as much works of art as they are quintessential culinary tools.

And he's right—sometimes it's hard to get past the beauty of a Cosmo knife to realize that it exists to do what that stone chunk in the British museum—the most basic tool man ever made—was created to do. To cut. Go to Burton's website, www.cosmoknives.com, and click on the video that shows Burton slicing through three hanks of inch-thick hemp rope lashed together, suspended. The knife goes through them like a laser through butter. In one swipe.

Makes you wish the paleolithic artisan sweating over his chipped rocks in that African gorge a couple of million years ago could see what he started.

Saskatchewan Floyd

This a story about Saskatchewan Floyd. I don't know his full name but that's what he's known as down at the coffee shop. Rangy kind of guy, thirty, maybe forty, carrot-coloured hair, smiles a lot, walks on the balls of his feet. Showed up on a spring day a couple of years ago in a beater Ford pickup with rusted fender wells, a block heater cord sticking out of the grill and Saskatchewan plates. Said his name was Floyd and he was looking for work.

Nobody said anything out loud at the time, but I think a lot of us placed our personal subconscious bets on how long Saskatchewan Floyd was going to last.

Prairie people don't always fare as well as they should on Salt Spring. Oh, they handle the summers fine—who wouldn't? It's like the Mediterranean here. But then there's the other ten months of the year, which lean toward grey. And wet. All that downfalling moisture tends to erode the esprit de corps of somebody raised under the big sky and blazing sunshine of Saskatoon or Swift Current or Brandon.

Actually, the winters get to a lot of Salt Springers, native and otherwise. That's why each fall there's a mass migration from these shores—not just hummingbirds, Canada geese and robins and finches—featherless Salt Springers too. They borrow the wings of United and Alaska Airlines, Air Canada and WestJet and take off for Malaque, Manzanilla and Maui, where the living is easy, sunny and dry.

Some of us don't migrate of course. We have to stay home and work. Like Saskatchewan Floyd, who surprised us. He was still here the next spring and the spring after that. He was still driving his beater pickup but the Saskatchewan plates had disappeared and BC plates had taken their place. Now three, maybe four years later, he's a fixture down at the coffee shop most mornings before he goes off to work at whatever he does.

I was behind him in the coffee lineup the other day, about the third straight day of rain we had. I asked him how he was doing with the weather. His eyes lit up, he laughed, went into a squat and drew a circle with his forefinger about a metre across on the coffee shop floor.

"Back in Maple Creek," he said, "if we were out on a job and the sky turned dark we'd draw a circle like that in the dust.

"Soon as we counted thirty-five drops of rain in that circle, we were gone. We didn't work in the rain. Hell, it was so dry out there our tools would disintegrate in the rain." He shook his head. "First winter I spent in Vancouver, we had fifty-nine straight days of rain."

I asked him, how come he stuck it out? How come he was still here? "Well, it wasn't easy at first," said Saskatchewan Floyd. "I'd heard about depression but I'd never really experienced it. Then a friend of mine said I should get into gardening. I did. And it's made all the difference."

I said that gardens didn't do much better in a Salt Spring winter than folks from the Prairies do. Gardens turn brown, lose their leaves, go dormant.

"Not mine," said Saskatchewan Floyd. "I ain't got but one plant in a pot. I keep it in the living room. Under a grow light. Every morning before I go to work I get down on my knees beside that plant, I look right into that grow light and I say, 'Come on, Mary Jane, grow—you can do it.' I don't know how the plant's gonna turn out but I feel great."

Saskatchewan Floyd and his one-plant grow op. I think he's gonna fit right in.

How Old Is "Old"?

When I read the details of the survey my first thought was: what would Satchel say?

Satchel being Leroy Robert "Satchel" Paige, possibly the greatest pitcher ever to throw a baseball. Joe DiMaggio said he was the best he ever faced; Bob Feller said likewise. Hack Wilson, a power hitter from the same era, said a ball thrown by Paige "looked like a marble" when it crossed the plate. Paige had names for his pitches—Bat Dodger, Midnight Creeper, Midnight Rider, Jump Ball, Trouble Ball—but the experts say they all really came down to one pitch, a near-warp-speed fastball that batters could hardly see much less hit.

We'll never know just how good Paige was because he was a black man, barred by the colour of his skin from Major League baseball for most of his career. He didn't break the Major League colour barrier until he was old enough to be retired. But Paige wasn't ready to retire. He became the oldest rookie to play in the Bigs, debuting with the Cleveland Browns at the age of forty-two.

Paige simply refused to act his age. He played like a teenager, bouncing around the so-called Negro Leagues for decades. He also played ball in Cuba, Mexico, Puerto Rico and the Dominican Republic before finally putting in nearly twenty years in the majors. He started his pro career in 1926. He was still fanning batters for the Kansas City Athletics in 1965.

It's a pity Satchel's gone to his reward because I'm pretty sure he would have had a belly laugh if he'd seen the survey I mentioned earlier. It was a telephone poll of 2,969 Americans conducted by the Pew Research Center, a Washington DC "fact tank." The main question the survey posed: how old is old?

Not surprisingly, the answer turns out to be—it depends who you ask. Respondents who were born around the Second World War opined that "old age" commences at about age eighty-one. Baby boomers thought it was closer to seventy-seven. Generation Xers, whose birth year falls between 1964 and 1970, expected to get doddery around the age of seventy-one, while Generation Yers, a.k.a. the Millennials—that's what they're calling pups born in the 1980s and 1990s—figured they'd start losing it about the age of sixty-two.

I'd snort, except I can remember back in the '60s hearing a California student activist shout into a bullhorn, "DON'T TRUST ANYONE OVER THIRTY!"

And I remember thinking: Yeah, that sounds about right.

I was approximately twenty at the time.

Satchel Paige? He was around in the early '60s, too, still winning ball games as a closing pitcher for the Kansas City Athletics.

By coincidence, Paige was in his early sixties as well. The man simply would not act his age.

He didn't just baffle batters. Paige also drove sports reporters nuts by adamantly refusing to reveal his birthdate. When cornered for the umpteenth time by a newshound asking the age-old old-age question, an exasperated Paige retorted, "How old would you be, if you didn't know how old you was?"

Shaky grammar; rock-solid philosophy.

Can't Lose If You Don't Buy a Ticket

My friend Arnie is an investment speculator. Every time he buys a pack of Marlboros he scoops up a handful of lottery tickets as well. "I figure it's only a matter of time," he says.

Did I mention my friend Arnie is an optimist? Subspecies delusional? Any Vegas gambler could tell him he's got a better chance of dying from cigarette-induced lung cancer than winning a lottery jackpot, but Arnie isn't looking for reality; he's Dreaming the Dream.

Still, chasing moonbeams is better than catching one. Buying lottery tickets is a harmless-enough waste of time, the real trouble starts when you win. Ask Jack Whittaker.

Unfortunately it would cost you fifteen thousand dollars just to ask Jack Whittaker the time of day. That's what Whittaker charges now to talk publicly to anyone. Not that anyone's lining up to pay.

Jack Whittaker doesn't need the money. He knows all about winning lotteries. He's the king. On Christmas Eve back in 2002 he bought a one-dollar Powerball ticket at a convenience store in West Virginia. He woke up the next morning to discover he had just won the jackpot—$315.

Followed by six zeros.

Did it change his life? Well, I guess. He was already a moderately wealthy man with a plumbing business and over a hundred employees, but still. Three hundred and fifteen million dollars . . .

Actually, after taxes and opting for a one-time payout rather than thirty years of instalments, Whittaker's take withered to about ninety-three million dollars—but hey!

First thing, Whittaker gave a hundred thousand dollars to the owner of the convenience store where he bought the ticket. Then he bought a brand new Jeep for the clerk who sold him the ticket. And what the hell? He wrote her a cheque for $123,000 so she could buy a house too.

Ninety-three million dollars? Whoo-ee! He donated seven million dollars to build two churches; another fourteen million dollars to the Jack Whittaker Foundation, to help the needy. He paid for a Little League park to be built. He bought himself a helicopter, sent his wife on a trip to the Holy Land and bought his beloved granddaughter Brandi not just one new car but five of them.

The money brought a lot of changes to Jack Whittaker's life. It also fostered attitudinal changes. Whittaker had always been a flamboyant party guy in his trademark Stetson and braying laugh. Ninety-three million dollars ramped "flamboyant" up to "obnoxious" and "party guy" to "troublesome drunk." He got arrested. A lot. Mostly for drunk driving but also for disorderly conduct and unlawful possession of firearms. His reaction was always the same. "It doesn't bother me because I can tell everyone to kiss off. I won the lottery."

His wife of forty-two years did kiss off, filing for divorce after Whittaker had been exposed too many times in too many strip clubs next to women who weren't Mrs. Whittaker. His former friends drifted away too, replaced by foxy ladies, good-time Charlies and other riff-raff of the leech persuasion.

For Jack Whittaker, everything went south after he won the lottery. Even his beloved granddaughter Brandi turned sullen and bitter. As the favourite relative of the biggest lottery winner in history, she also became a magnet for opportunistic low-lifes. At sixteen Brandi went into rehab to treat her addiction to hillbilly heroin—OxyContin. In 2004, barely two years after Whittaker's win, Brandi's drug-riddled body was discovered wrapped in a plastic tarp and stuffed behind a junk car.

Jack heard about it over the phone. He was in rehab for alcohol addiction at the time.

Now it's ten years later and Whittaker, surveying the ruins of his life, says he wishes he could travel back in time to tear up that ticket and throw away the pieces.

Good deal for the folks who run the Powerball lottery though. They made sure the papers and TV stations got great photos of Jack receiving the monster cheque; and of Jack riding through New York City in a stretch limo; and of Jack and his wife, Jewel, being interviewed on the *Today* show the morning after. That's the kind of publicity that sells a lot of lottery tickets.

As for Jack's business, his marriage, his health, his dead grand-daughter, well . . .

What was that phrase the US military used to use when they accidentally bombed a few Vietnamese or Afghani or Iraqi civilians?

Oh, right: collateral damage.

PART FOUR

Home Sweet Salt Spring

No Shirt, No Shoes, No Cell Service

You know what I think is the very best thing about living on Salt Spring? Cellphone reception. It's terrible on the island—well, on big chunks of the island anyway. A lot of first-time visitors arriving by ferry at the south end are mystified by what I call the Fulford Fandango. It's not uncommon at the ferry dock in Fulford Harbour to see some citizens whirling around in circles holding their hands to their heads as if they've got intense headaches. They aren't members of some bizarre Sufi cult and they're not in pain. They are real estate agents who've suddenly lost their cell connection to a client. If you get close enough you'll hear their telltale, plaintive cry: CAN'T HEAR YOU, YOU'RE BREAKING UP! CAN'T HEAR YOU, YOU'RE BREAKING UP!

Much of Salt Spring Island is enveloped in a black hole, or, as I prefer to think of it, a Cathedral of Quiet that deflects wireless transmissions and renders most cellphones utterly useless or at least unreliable.

Unfortunately this blessed cell-free zone disappears just a few hundred yards off shore of Salt Spring Island. If you're on a BC Ferry coming to or leaving the island, reception is just fine. Which means you can be sure your ferry nap will be interrupted by a one-sided conversation that will go something like this:

HI, HONEY. IT'S ME, FRED. Everybody in the lounge, whether they're reading or relaxing or just trying to nap, glares at Fred. He doesn't notice. YEAH. JUST COMING IN TO TSAWWASSEN

NOW. YEAH, I KNOW I WAS SUPPOSED TO BE ON THE 3:30 BUT I WORKED LATE. NO, I DIDN'T GO TO THE OFFICE PARTY. I AM NOT SLURRING. I AM NOT CALLING FROM SOME MOTEL LOBBY I'M ON THE SPIRIT OF BRITISH COLUMBIA FERRY! OF COURSE I LOVE YOU. OF COURSE THERE'S NO ONE ELSE.

Personally I've never known what to do about guys like Fred on their cellphones. My crocodile brain says to grab him by his tie and the seat of his pants and throw him into the Salish Sea, but that would mean complications. And possible jail time. I've considered telling Fred to shut the hell up, but sometimes Fred is larger and younger than me and that would mean complications. And possible hospital time.

I like the way the lady who was sitting right next to Fred handled it. Fred was just explaining over the phone that BABY BELIEVE ME THERE'S NO ONE ELSE. YOU'RE MY ITTY BITTY SNUGGLE BUNNY BABY when the lady sitting next to him leaned over toward Fred and his cell and said in her sexiest voice. "Come on, Fred, stop talking on the phone and come back to bed."

Sure hope Fred's reception died before Snuggle Bunny heard that.

The Daily Grind

You know why most people never move to the Gulf Islands? The economy. Sure. Once you've made the decision, quit your Mainland job, hopped the ferry with all your worldly goods crammed into the trunk and strapped onto the roof of your Chevy Nova—once you're on the island, what are you going to do? To support yourself, I mean?

Oh, it's no problem for the dot-com gazillionaires, the semi-retired rock stars and the superannuated Calgary oil executives—but that's about .0014 percent of the population. What about the rest of us?

The Gulf Islands are not Silicon Valley. There are no auto plants or pulp mills on Texada or Denman. No Wall or Bay or Howe Street financial districts. We don't even have big box stores or McDonald's.

So what does an average Gulf Islander do to put in his or her time? I can answer that. We drink coffee.

Drinking coffee is unquestionably the prime Gulf Island pastime, certainly on Salt Spring, where I live.

Mind you, I'm using the term "coffee" loosely here. Individual Salt Springers may drink cappuccinos, soy lattes, Americanos or powdered Nescafé in a Dixie cup. They may also opt for jasmine tea, Walla Walla blend organic betel chai, steamed Mango Essence Surprise or Mother Parkers instant . . . but one way or another, Gulf Islanders spend an inordinate amount of time sitting around sucking hot-ish caffeinated liquids out of cups.

Which makes the Slurp industry about as close to a Big Business as the Gulf Islands get. Not long after I landed here, I heard that some acquaintances were planning to open a new coffee shop downtown. Now, my name's Arthur, not Conrad. I don't pretend to have a lot of business sense. But even I, financial nincompoop that I am, recognize a doomed flight of kamikaze commerce when I trip over it. These folks were about to commit economic suicide.

They planned to open a coffee house about fifty feet from Barb's Buns, a very popular watering hole, and, from fifty feet in the other direction, a place called Moka House—also a major hangout for island caffeine freaks. Plus the new establishment would be less than a sugar cube toss from at least a half-dozen other cafés, bistros, diners and beaneries—all of which already served a more than decent cuppa java.

Were they nuts? No question. Did they listen to my warnings? No. They went right ahead and opened a place called Roasters. And today? Well, today, if you go in real early you might get a seat at Roasters. If you leave it too late you'll join the tail of the takeout line coming out the front door.

Roasters fared so poorly that pretty soon they opened another Roasters at the far end of the island. Which gave them the same number of Salt Spring outlets as Canada Post. And twice as many as the local constabulary.

So coffee houses are big business on the islands—but the fact is most of us are not cut out to be coffee shop owners. We don't fly that high. Our job is to hold up the other end of the caffeine equation— namely to drink the product.

And I'm not pretending that it's an easy or lucrative way to spend your life. This is no nine-to-five, union-padded gig we're talking about here. Coffee drinkers don't get covered under any special dental plan or extended health benefit scheme. The hours are brutal and we don't get six-week vacations or a chance to buy shares in the company. The lowliest sales peon in the backwardest used car lot in the province gets a desk, a phone, a computer and all the paper clips he or she can lift. In my line of work, you're lucky if you get a coffee card.

I'm not complaining. I'm merely pointing out that caffeine is to the Gulf Islands what crude oil is to Alberta. It's the lifeblood that makes this economy work.

And we coffee drinkers, we're the spud men and the roughnecks that get that caffeine out of the espresso machines and into the public bloodstream where it belongs.

So, no fanfare—we don't expect that. But a little respect would be nice. Next time you see a professional coffee drinker hunched over his or her double soy macchiato . . . a little smile . . . perhaps even a casual salute. They're ruining their kidneys for you. In the immortal words of Churchill (that would be Randolph, not Winston): "They also serve who only slouch and slurp."

Geese: Not for the Faint-Hearted

Travis says he knows exactly what we oughtta do with them. (Travis hasn't been on Salt Spring long but he's from Toronto so he always knows what we oughtta do about things.)

"Just pop 'em," says Travis. "Shoot 'em, pluck 'em, cook 'em and eat 'em.

"Shoot one of those big boys, feed a family of six. Hell—shoot a couple dozen and feed the island's homeless."

It's geese Travis is talking about. *Branta canadensis*. The Canada goose. They are a nuisance here, for sure. They gatecrash our meadows, party loud in our bays and lagoons, take over our school yards and parks, pluck our soccer fields bare . . . but most of all, they poop. Man, do they poop. Scientists report—and I don't want to know how they found this out—that the average adult Canada goose poops up to ninety-two times a day. Multiply that by the hundreds upon hundreds of geese that call Salt Spring home and . . . well, point made.

It would be dreary enough if this was just a domestic problem, but these poop machines are our goodwill ambassadors to the rest of the world. Years ago, before the fecal fecundity of these birds was fully appreciated, our diplomats gave mating pairs to Argentina, to Russia and to Great Britain.

They still haven't forgiven us. "The Canada goose," sniffed a recent editorial in the *Daily Mail*, "is one of Britain's most hated birds."

They also, of course, fly south annually by the millions. And they don't give a fig for Homeland Security. The Americans have noticed. Last year they gunned down two million of them. In New York City and Nassau County alone, authorities culled two thousand.

Which kind of underlines Travis's point of, um, culling two birds with one stone by shooting them and cooking up the carcasses to feed the homeless.

There's just one small problem: Salt Spring's Canada geese should never be confused with the grain-fed butterballs that mainland Canada knows. Our Canada geese are seabirds. They breed and nest and feed in the waters of the Pacific Ocean. And they taste like it.

I know a guy who tried to cook an island goose. He put it in the oven for the better part of a day. Showered it with herbs and spices, massaged it with tasty oils and gastronomic unguents. Served it up to his family. The verdict: stringy, dry and tasting like the inside of an otter's armpit.

Oscar Wilde once dismissed the British tradition of the fox hunt by calling it "the unspeakable in pursuit of the uneatable."

I can't imagine what he'd have to say about a drumstick from an island Canada goose.

Remembering Names? I'm a Bust

The man had a weathered, prairie gruffness about him. The lines on his face were carved into a permanent frown and the coals of his eyes blazed out from under a wiry tangle of iron-grey, bushy brow.

He looked—formidable. But he possessed a gift that endeared him to almost everyone he met.

He remembered you.

Not just you, but your spouse's name, how many kids you had, where you lived and how much land you owned.

"Jake Winters, how are you?" he would say, with a handshake and a searchlight glare that swept the dark corners of your soul. "How's Eunice? Did she have that knee fixed? Got your crop in?"

A chap could parlay a talent like that into a profitable career in sales, the ministry, the media. Or politics.

This particular chap chose the latter. His name was John George Diefenbaker.

No matter how you felt about his politics, you had to admire the man who became our thirteenth prime minister. He had mastered the fundamental rule of civilized behaviour: really, really care about your neighbours. Your neighbours will get it, and they will never forget you.

Other cultures get it. The Japanese bow to strangers; the Hawaiians welcome you ashore with a sultry song and dance. On Salt Spring Island, the natives greet you with a bear hug, doesn't matter if you're Matt Damon or the local dogcatcher.

We could all use a hug—or at the very least, we could acknowledge each other more with smiles than with studied indifference. As a country mouse kind of guy I'm always struck when I venture to the big city by the lack of eye contact. Urban types usually look away if you try to catch their eye, and I understand that, I guess. Where I live, I'm lucky to run into twenty people a day. If I took the Toronto subway to just one Maple Leafs hockey game I'd see thousands and thousands of faces in a single evening.

And that's for a Leafs game—just imagine if Toronto had an actual hockey team.

Dolly Parton, I am told, frequently has to deal with male fans who become utterly tongue-tied and speechless when confronted by Dolly's twin Icebreakers. She's found a way to break the ice, as it were. Dolly smiles, puts her arms around the flustered fan's neck and mashes his bashful mug deep into her cleavage.

Not such a good tactic for me, of course. If I mashed somebody into my cleavage I'd probably break their nose.

What's a guy to do? I'd like to make my encounters more memorable, but it's not as if I look like Ryan Gosling, dress like Don Cherry, sing like Michael Bublé or write like Leonard Cohen.

The Diefenbaker option is out. My memory's too porous to remember the names of the people I meet, much less their families, their acreage and their medical history—at least that's what my Life Partner, old what's-her-name, says.

But I am finally doing something about it. I've signed up for a correspondence course on how to remember names and faces. In fact, it's number two on my bucket list.

Number one is getting invited to meet Dolly Parton.

Hookers on Salt Spring

A lot of writers have written a lot of articles about Salt Spring Island. They write about our artists and our craftspeople; they write about our hippies and our yuppies; our friendly open market and our vicious Taliban-style politics.

Nobody ever writes about our Salt Spring hookers.

Oh yeah. Salt Spring is not some rustic puritanical, Bible-belt backwater, you know. We've got our hookers, all right. There's Janet and June and Mary and Yvette, Irene and Sandy and Barb and Mary, Anne and Gladys and Marlene and Marilyn, Donna and Lynne and Lori and the other Mary.

Those are just the ones I know personally. Heck one of them— Lynne—I've been sleeping with her regularly for the past thirty-odd years.

Oh I know the Salt Spring hookers all right. And I know they're all pretty tired of all the lame jokes (like this extended one) about their chosen pastime.

It's rug hooking we're talking about. A craft that's at least two hundred years old, going back to the early nineteenth century in Yorkshire, England, where workers in the weaving mills were allowed to collect thrums, or scraps of yarn left over after the weaving process.

The workers took the thrums home and figured out a way to push them through a backing material, which produced primitive rugs to warm the floors of their hovels.

The basics of rug hooking haven't changed a whole lot since those early days. Hookers still take scraps of material cut into various widths and drag them through a piece of burlap using a thick needle with a barb or hook on the end of it to catch and pull the cloth through. But the artistic component has blossomed.

Rug hooking is not easy; it's not quick—and it's not that common. Especially in these times when you can go to a big box store and order your factory-made carpet by the yard.

But that's one of the attractions of rug hooking. The end product is everything a factory-made rug is not. It's personal and it's handmade with love. Good hookers can render spectacular landscapes, seascapes, floral arrays, abstract patterns, geometric panoramas and astonishingly evocative portraits of loved ones, two- and four-legged. And they do it with a patient artistry that can make you catch your breath.

They don't do it for the money and they don't do it for fame. They do it for the camaraderie, the fellowship and the history . . . because hooked rugs tell stories and they endure, even when—some say especially when—they're walked on.

Modern technology and the Industrial Revolution almost sent rug hooking the way of calligraphy and spittoon making but there's a resurgence going on. Rug hooking groups are springing up in Australia and Europe, in Mexico and Central America; and in places like the Canadian Maritimes, Newfoundland and Labrador and the US eastern seaboard they never really went away.

I know of active hooker enclaves in Victoria, Nanaimo and Parksville—and that's just in my neck of the BC woods.

Personally, I like the slogan of a group of practitioners in the town of Agustin Gonzalez, Mexico. Its slogan? "Have you kissed a hooker today?"

I know I've done my part.

It's a Jungle Out Here

Another winter. I've been here before. I've passed winters in the Atlas mountains of North Africa and the boggy suburbs of London, England; I've shivered through winters in Quebec, in PEI and in Ontario, north and south—but the flat-out weirdest winters I've ever gone through are right here on Salt Spring Island.

Un-winters, really. The place never stops being green. Several shades of green. They're darker than your spring and summer greens— but green! Tell that to somebody in Thunder Bay trying to get their car engine to turn over on a minus 40 degree morning. And something vegetative is always pumping out new growth here, every month of the year. Bizarre bushes I've never seen before popping blossoms in December, shedding leaves in March. That kind of thing doesn't happen in Yellowknife or Corner Brook. Or Edmonton or Toronto.

I'll tell you another thing that doesn't happen too often in a Canadian winter. It's the thing that happened to me the other morning. I'm out on my front porch to get some wood for the fire and suddenly there's an outboard motorboat revving by my ear.

It wasn't an outboard motorboat; it was an Anna's hummingbird. A smidge of iridescent feathers about the size of your thumb that weighs as much as that quarter in your pocket. Alive and foraging in Canada. At the end of November.

I thought I was hallucinating but it turns out it's true—this one species of the family of the world's smallest bird does overwinter in the nethermost regions of British Columbia. They haven't been doing it for long—Arizona and California are their preferred wintering grounds. The first recorded Great White North sighting occurred in the 1950s just north of Victoria. Experts estimate there are maybe five to six hundred nesting females on Vancouver Island and the Lower Mainland. And in case you're wondering who Anna was, she was a nineteenth-century duchess. Anna Massena, the Duchess of Rivoli.

Cynics say there's no such thing as miracles but is it not just slightly miraculous that I could have a hummingbird thrumming at my ear in Canada at the end of November?

Close enough for me. I know what that hummer was after, too—the feeder that I took down six weeks ago because I thought all the hummingbirds had gone south. Hummingbirds are tiny but they aren't meek. The bird was buzzing me to tell me to get with the program.

Point taken. The hummingbird feeder is out there again, full of hummingbird nectar—three parts water to one part sugar. It could freeze, of course. Salt Spring winters are mild but this ain't Honolulu. So I take it in last thing at night and put it out before dawn. No return visits yet, but what the heck? It isn't even Christmas. And that's just early spring to an Anna's hummingbird.

Island Hopping

How unlikely is this? I'm sitting in a rec centre in the middle of a Gulf Island in the middle of the afternoon of a Canadian winter day when four women with flowers in their hair, one of them strumming a ukulele, weave down the aisle in muumuus bedecked with garlands of flowers, singing . . . Hawaiian love songs?

It happened. And I wasn't dreaming, drinking or ingesting dubious chemicals.

It wasn't all that unusual when you think about it—this is Salt Spring Island, after all. And if we're not the national melting pot we're at least the tossed salad of the Canada.

We live here at the behest of First Nations people who called this island home for at least a couple of millennia before we showed up. And even before Canada was a country we had substantial black settlements from one end of the island to the other. In 1895 a Victoria newspaper reported that Salt Spring was inhabited by "160 English, 50 Scots, 20 Irish, 22 Portuguese, 13 Swedes, 2 Norwegians, 34 Americans, 10 Japanese, 1 Egyptian, 2 Germans, 1 Patagonian," and, according to the reporter, "90 half breeds and 40 coloured." Unquote. No political correctness in 1895.

Ah, but there's one group of Salt Springers on the list that you wouldn't find in many parts of Canada then or now. Between the ten Japanese and the one Egyptian the report speaks of six "Sandwich Islanders."

Those would be Hawaiians. And that would be the reason for the six women swaying down the aisle of the recreation centre with flowers in their hair and a Hawaiian love song on their lips.

Hawaiians—Kanakas they are called here—are alive and well on Salt Spring. Have been since the mid-1800s when their ancestors came here to work as contract labourers for the Hudson's Bay Company fur traders. The Kanakas were—are—versatile and talented people. The fur trade died but the Kanakas diversified—fishing, farming, logging, construction—even politics. Mel Couvelier, who was once BC's finance minister, was a Kanaka descendant of the Mahoi and Douglas families of Salt Spring.

By and large, though, Salt Spring's Kanaka community was a pretty well-kept secret—until 1970 when a Hawaiian newspaper got wind of it. The *Honolulu Advertiser* turned what it called The Lost Hawaiians into a front-page story. It teamed up with CP Air to fly a whole raft of Salt Spring Kanakas to Hawaii free of charge, where they were wined and dined and introduced to a princess of the Hawaiian royal family who embraced them and asked, "Why have you been gone so long?"

"Well, Princess," said one of the Salt Springers, "we didn't realize you were looking for us."

That's how the Kanakas stay alive and well on Salt Spring. They sing their songs; they dance their dances. They keep their stories alive. And just when you're not expecting it, they give you a playful poke in the ribs.

The Naked Truth

en years ago, a war broke out on Salt Spring. The People versus Texada Land Corporation, an Alberta-based consortium, and the bone of contention was five thousand acres of pristine, undeveloped Salt Spring forest. The stakes were high and simple: Texada wanted to clear-cut the land and sell off the bald lots. The people thought not.

The war was fought in all the usual ways that non-shooting wars go. Sit-ins. Rallies. Songs were sung, speeches were made, letters were written, politicians were poked to see if they could be dislodged from their fences. Mort Ransen, the filmmaker who gave us *Margaret's Museum* and a long-time resident of the island, put out a hilarious, biting documentary called *The Money, The Money, The Money* (which was the explanatory mantra actually chanted by one of the Texada owners when asked why a Calgary company had the hots for Salt Spring timber—but I digress).

All the usual protest bases were covered but there was a serious lack of cash. Protests cost money. How to raise it? Someone said: Why not put out a calendar? Why not . . . a nude calendar?

Sounds pretty mundane now—nude calendars for charity are a dime a dozen these days—but a decade ago, this was provocative stuff. And Salt Spring was pretty much a perfect springboard for a nude calendar. For one thing, the island had Howard Fry, an internationally famous fashion photographer, lately retired, who was willing to lend his talents. For another thing, the island had the, uh, requisite natural resources for a nude calendar. Beautiful women. Lots of them. Too many, in fact, for a mere twelve-month calendar, as it turned out. In the end, thirty-seven amateur but passionate models made the final cut. They were photographed by island lakes, in island farmyards, on island mountaintops and peeping out of island old growth. All natural surroundings and all *au naturel*.

Was it successful? It was a sensation. The story was picked up by the *Vancouver Sun*, then *The Globe and Mail*, then *Harper's Magazine*. Popular, too. Over a hundred thousand dollars was raised from calendar sales. Which contributed significantly to the successful resolution of the Salt Spring/Texada Corp. war. The Calgary developers were sent packing (albeit with a fat cheque in their carpetbag); the land was saved and covenanted against future depredation. As a matter of fact, I took my dogs for a walk through part of it the other morning. Saw one blue heron, two eagles, a family of otters, several deer . . . and zero logging trucks.

Pecha Kucha Power

So I get this phone call one evening and a voice I don't recognize says, "Arthur, we'd like to invite you to a special event next Friday. It's a PATCHOOKACHA!"

"Gesundheit," I say into the phone.

My bad. The lady wasn't suffering from hay fever, she was inviting me to a Pecha Kucha. A very specialized presentation night, where a few selected people from various walks of life get to talk about their passion in a strictly controlled format.

Pecha Kucha, a Japanese term because that's where the idea began, means approximately "sound of chit-chat." Here's how it works: People get together in a space. It can be a living room, a town hall, a community centre—mine happened in a barn—and they mix and mingle. Presently, the formal part of the evening begins. A speaker gets up and talks about his or her passion, while slides are shown on a screen. Here's what makes it Pecha Kucha and not an evening of crashing boredom. Each presenter has exactly twenty slides to illustrate their presentation. Each slide is shown for exactly twenty seconds (there's a timer on the projector). This means nobody gets to talk for more (or less) than six minutes and forty seconds.

You will not fall asleep at a Pecha Kucha get-together.

There were six presenters at the Pecha Kucha night I attended. An island chef spoke of the circular equation that rules his life: Food is Love is Food. There was a photographer who doubles as a house

136

and pet sitter. Her presentation was a series of photographs called "I Woke Up Here." She took photos each day for years to, as she put it, remember where she'd been. We heard from a man whose passion is BC's spectacular answer to the cactus—the living fossil that's known as the monkey puzzle tree. We heard from a woman who sculpts in native island stone, and from a potter who tries to emulate the lines and forms of nature in clay. And we heard from a school principal whose passion is the children who mine the biggest, most dangerous resource site in all of the Americas—the garbage dump outside Guatemala City.

We heard all six presenters—each one for exactly six minutes and forty seconds—and then we all got up to mix and mingle again to talk about what we'd seen and heard and felt.

And it was fabulous. It was like a cocktail party that actually works. That barn was crackling with energy and creative spark. Which apparently is how it goes with Pecha Kucha. The phenomenon is going viral. That first Pecha Kucha night in Tokyo in 2003 has led to Pecha Kucha nights in 417 different towns and cities all around the globe including Vancouver, Victoria, Whistler and Salt Spring. One of the many great things about Pecha Kucha—aside from the fact that there's no admission charge, it's exciting as hell and it leaves you feeling super-charged as a teenager, only smarter—is the fact that it's democratic. No need to rent the Rogers Arena or bring in big-name, expensive presenters. That's top-down stuff. Pecha Kucha is bottom-up. Those are your friends and neighbours up there talking about their passions. If you want to find out more, just google "PKN." That'll get you there, eventually.

And remember, the next time you're on a bus or in an elevator or standing in a lineup and someone behind you goes, "ah . . . ah . . . ptchKOOcha!"

Don't say gesundheit. Say, "Oh! Can I come, too?"

Whale Watching

We get a lot of tourists on Salt Spring in the summertime. They come in by ferry or by private boat or by seaplane so it really shouldn't have been all that noteworthy to see the party of six that came in by water a couple of weekends ago. They stopped off for lunch at Second Sister Island, then continued on into Ganges Harbour, probably to check out our Saturday market, as so many tourists do.

The lunch they had at Second Sister Island was, um, seal. Raw seal. The tourists? A pod of transient killer whales.

I knew something was up when I saw the red and black Zodiacs full of pink faces clustered together out in Long Harbour. Those boats belong to whale-watching companies in Victoria that exist to track down pods of orca and then transport boatloads of tourists to see them.

Call me Eeyore but I find it kind of sad, the whole whale-watching business. They use land spotters and boat spotters cruising in Zodiacs that can hit fifty or sixty knots. The animals are even tracked by satellite, so there's really nowhere to hide.

The Coast Guard did a good job looking out for the Salt Spring visitors. They made several marine broadcasts reminding the rubber-neckers that they were watching an endangered species and to stay clear.

The rules say that no boats are to harass or get within a hundred metres of an orca, but an orca's sense of hearing has to be ultra-sensitive—they navigate by echolocation. Have you ever heard an outboard motor with your head under water? Even to a human ear a hundred yards away, it would sound like a chainsaw parked on your shoulder.

It's a double-edged sword. Sleek and lithe and long as a bus, up to nine tons in weight, the orca moves like a ballerina. It is a wonder of nature, and people should get to be wonderstruck by the majesty of these creatures. But if we mess them up through intrusive gawking, what's the profit?

Still, on the bright side, all those people ARE just gawking at the orcas; they're not shooting them, or capturing them to turn them into entertainment clowns in pens like SeaWorld in California or MarineLand in Niagara Falls. That wasn't true less than a generation ago.

And I'm happy to report that the machine gun at the entrance to Pender Harbour is gone. Not making that up. Less than a generation ago, orcas in BC waters were shot for sport. And as recently as 1960 there was a machine gun at Pender and others elsewhere in the Georgia Strait. Purpose: to, ahem, cull orcas. Government-approved, too. It was thought that they were "costing us money" by eating too many salmon.

There's an old Cree proverb that goes: "Until you catch the last fish, until you cut the last tree, until you poison the last river, then and only then will you understand that money cannot be eaten."

The Harper government has recently "streamlined" the environmental assessment process for all of Canada. "Streamlined" means that nearly 90 percent of existing environmental assessment agencies have been evaporated. Government says the move will attract significant investment dollars.

No comment from the environment.

Hollywood North? Don't Believe It

Big trouble on the Rock—Salt Spring I mean. The island's been found out, exposed. Caught in the high beams, spread-eagled on our face and pinned to the page like a butterfly in a lepidopterological specimen book.

A feature article in a magazine put out by American Airways has declared Salt Spring "one of Canada's best-kept secrets."

Bad enough. But in the same week Yahoo Travel, an online service that caters to tourists worldwide, named Salt Spring "one of the World's Ten Most Secret Islands." We're right up there with, um, Madeline Island in Lake Superior.

Madeline Island as a secret I can believe. I never heard of it—and I lived in Thunder Bay on the shores of Lake Superior for thirteen years.

But Salt Spring? Secret??? From whom? Salt Spring's been featured in the travel pages of *The Globe and Mail* and the *Toronto Star*, not to mention the *New York* and *Los Angeles Times*. Calling Salt Spring a secret is like calling Don Cherry an introvert.

No, Salt Spring's well known all right—a little too well known to suit many old-timers. In fact Salt Spring's newsworthiness has created a kind of perverse subcult on the island. I call them the celeb junkies. These islanders live to report and gossip about celebrity sightings on the island.

For instance did you know that Barbra Streisand was seen

sunbathing in a bikini on the front deck of her yacht in Ganges Harbour last summer?

That Stan Lam once blasted a customer at his convenience store who was leafing through the latest issue of the *Gulf Islands Driftwood* at the news rack instead of buying it? Turned out the mooch customer was Al Pacino.

That a holy mystic from India personally blessed this island from a passing airplane because he sensed a glowing crystal under Mount Tuam? That Robin Williams has a secret hundred-acre ranch in the south end?

Are any of these stories true? Nah. But hundreds believe them. I have a standing offer of a quarter pound of heavenly ash-ripened camembert from Moonstruck Organic Cheese to the first person who shows me incontrovertible proof that Robin Williams ever flew over Salt Spring much less maintains a secret hideaway here—but so far, no takers.

Nope, Salt Spring is a lot of things, but being a secret isn't one of them. And neither is being a hideout for Hollywood pinups.

When it comes to hams, hustlers, has-beens and hopefuls with big hooters—we do homegrown here. We don't need to import.

Another Perfect Day in Paradise

One question that I get to field a lot is: "What's it like to live on Salt Spring Island? Seriously." This question does not come from other Gulf Islanders, you understand. Folks on Pender and Saturna and Gabriola and Galiano lead a more peaceful and bucolic existence compared to the frenzied pace of Salt Spring with our . . . stop signs and our baristas and our . . . electricity and everything. That's why other Gulf Islanders don't refer to our island as Salt Spring. They call it Sodom by the Sea.

We can't win. To American tourists we're all loggers or hippies; to Vancouverites we're dope farmers or Hollywood Norma Desmond–style recluses.

The truth is, as is so often the case, a little more complex.

Trying to nail the essence of Salt Spring is like trying to catch a hummingbird in your hat. It shifts too fast. Zips here, darts there, hovers over yonder.

I could never give you the epic docudrama of life on this island, but I can offer you a snapshot.

Picture yourself sitting at a table, sipping a tall chai latte in the quaint and cosy Café Talia in downtown Ganges. Your perusal of cartoons in an old coffee-ringed café copy of the *New Yorker* is interrupted by a querulous, high-decibel gabble coming from the branches of a tall maple across the road. It's a huge flock of crows and they're cawing and flapping and swooping around . . . another crow. This crow is in distress, fluttering and flapping weakly in the high branches of the tree. Turns out he's entangled in a plastic bag and it's obviously strangling him.

What to do? Climbing the tree was out, though one young Tarzan tried it. He just couldn't get close enough to the bird. So . . . call the fire department; call the Wildlife Centre.

The wildlife rescue people come with nets and ladders but the crow is still out of reach, and now ominously inert. The call goes out for Wayne Langley, a tree-cutting (and -climbing) professional. Langley arrives festooned in harnesses and caribiners and hauling specialized tree-climbing equipment. He scales the tree like a squirrel commando and frees the bird. The bird flies off, picking up a squadron of crow companions, doubtless croaking in fluent crow-ese, "What just happened back there?"

What just happened? Typical day on Salt Spring is all. And Diana Hayes, an island poet who happened to be sitting in Café Talia during the rescue, has let it be known that she was inspired by the event and is attempting a sequel to the Wallace Stevens poem called "Thirteen Ways of Looking at a Blackbird." She's asking people to send her a stanza so that the poem can be a renga.

Me? I'm off to look up that Wallace Stevens poem. And to find out what "renga" means.

And that's what it's like to live on this island.

Small Differences; Big Problem

Sigmund Freud was a sour old bugger, but a smart guy for all that. He wrote about something he called the Narcissism of Small Differences.

That hits me where I live—Salt Spring Island.

Salt Spring is Narcissism Central; we thrive on small differences here. I was at a meeting once where a guy stood up and suggested a plan to deal with ferry traffic on the island. Somebody else stood up and said how much she resented newcomers coming to Salt Spring and telling us how to fix things. First guy said, "Wait a minute. I've been living on this island for twenty years." The woman replied, "Yeah—on the north end!"

Small differences. People in the know don't order a coffee on Salt Spring. They order a yerba latte macchiato soy decaf—and then they ask if the soybeans are free-range.

Salt Springers don't ask you if you want to party, they invite you to the Sacred Wiccan New Moon ceremony or an Ayurvedic Chakra Cleansing Rainbow weekend retreat.

But it isn't all fun and games on Salt Spring. We've got problems. In fact, we've got one major problem. Our problem is, there aren't enough problems on Salt Spring. We've got beautiful scenery, majestic eagles soaring overhead, photogenic deer munching the underbrush, no biting insects, hardly any politicians and the mildest weather in Canada.

The catch is—we're still Canadian. We're not used to bounty and ease. So we obsess over trivia.

Like, well, like potholes. Everybody who has roads has potholes sooner or later but if you believed the letters to the editor in the local paper, Salt Spring's been carpet-bombed by B-29s leaving craters big enough to swallow logging trucks. And those photogenic deer? A pestilence! A plague! They're destroying our rainforest ecosystem!

Not that anyone wants to hurt them of course. That would be bad karma.

Recently Salt Spring got its first four-way traffic stop. Two main roads intersect at right angles. Motorists are required to come to a halt, then proceed, using the well-known four-way stop procedure. Not exactly chaos theory or advanced metaphysics, one would think. The stop signs went in last year. People are still debating them.

And smart meters? Jeez, don't be mentioning smart meters over your yerba latte macchiato soy decaf. There are entire schools of theories on that one. The Chem Trail Hard-Liners are convinced it's a subversive tactic initiated by the military-industrial complex, while the New World Order Enthusiasts are dead certain a coalition of CIA, CSIS and Interpol is behind it.

Differences. Valdy said it first and best. Definition of Salt Spring, said Valdy: A difference of opinion surrounded by water.

We even have the French Question on Salt Spring. The question being: "How did those jumped-up *flâneurs* get to own the slogan '*Vive la différence*'?"

The French claim it, but here on Salt Spring, we live it! It should be emblazoned on our licence plates. SALT SPRING—VIVE LA DIFFÉRENCE.

There's a thought. We should sue France for copyright. I think I'll bring it up at the next town hall meeting.

Or maybe not. I've only been here fifteen years.

Double Trouble a-Brewing?

There was a significant earth tremor on Salt Spring this week. The epicentre was downtown Ganges but you could feel it as far as Beddis Beach and Fulford Harbour, too. I wasn't in town when it happened but I got there shortly after and the evidence was pretty irrefutable. It was a sign on the side of the building that used to be the gas station. "FUTURE HOME OF TIM HORTONS DRIVE THRU," it read. "FOR EMPLOYMENT ENQUIRIES CALL 1-888-601-1616."

Now for a lot of towns this would be welcome news. But we're talking Salt Spring here. Franchises do not flourish on Salt Spring. We don't have a Walmart or a Costco or a Best Buy or a London Drugs. A Pharmasave sneaked in but everybody needs a drug store and ours is one where everybody knows the pharmacist by her first name. We had a Dairy Queen for a minute and a half back in the '90s but it went out of business and was replaced by a flower store. It's kind of a snob thing. Not having a Taco Bell or a Wendy's helps preserve the fantasy that we live on a magic atoll that time forgot. But a Tim Hortons? On Salt Spring??

It's what you might call a double-double outrage, because if there's any place that doesn't need another coffee outlet, it's Salt Spring. The new Tim Hortons would be right across the street from TJ's coffee house. And just a couple of buildings away from the Roasting House coffee shop and Barb's Buns. And not much more than a coffee bean toss from the Talia Café and the Salt Spring Inn and the Tree House café and Auntie Pesto's and . . . hey, you can get a decent cup of coffee at our grocery store. How much coffee can one island drink?

I asked Busker Bob, one of our more dedicated caffeinatics, how he felt about a Tim Hortons in our future. He looked up at me under hooded eyes, like he was watching a long train of thought pass by and I was the caboose.

"You happen to notice what day the sign went up?" he asked softly. "Yeah," I said, "It was, uh, Tuesday, the first of the month."

"What month?" said Busker Bob softly.

"First of . . . Ap-ril," I said.

"Gotcha!" said Busker Bob.

Well, maybe. But the colours of the sign are Tim Hortons colours and I phoned 1-888-601-1616. It's Tim Horton's Headquarters. I spoke to Tara in Customer Relations. She'd never heard of Salt Spring Island, but she told me that's how the company opens a new outlet—a sign to let the public know what's going on. And, she added, "We don't do April Fool's pranks at Tim Hortons."

So there you go. I don't know if it's a prank or not. But if it is, it's the best one since the one about the Mount Belcher Spaghetti Tree harvest festival.

Tourism: Blessing or Curse?

Well, it's finally summer here on Salt Spring and it's not hard to tell. The tourists are back. We always have advance warning of the tourist arrival. It's invariably preceded by the Salt Spring grouse. That's not a bird. It's the sound of ten thousand Salt Springers mumbling, grumbling and, well, grousing.

"Damn tourists. Can't get anywhere, roads are clogged. No parking downtown. Had to make a reservation at Moby's last night . . ."

Ironic thing is, Salt Spring needs tourists like bears need the salmon run. The B&Bs, the hotels, a dozen or so restaurants, sports outfitters, the Saturday market, the Farmers' Market . . . They'd wither up and blow away without our annual tourist infusion. We have, for better or worse, a largely tourist-driven economy.

Not everyone begrudges the fact. A few years ago a *National Post* columnist airily declared that Vancouver Island and the Gulf Islands could easily accommodate a permanent population of ten or twenty million along with "millions of tourists every year."

I wouldn't argue. I'd just invite the columnist to spend a few days in Venice, Italy. That tiny and exquisite city gets sixty thousand tourists. Every. Single. Day. Nearly two million a year. They fly there, they drive there, but increasingly these days they arrive in cruise ships and on ferries. And by ferries I don't mean the *Queen of Nanaimo*. These Mediterranean ferries are seven hundred feet long and five decks high. Each one can disgorge five thousand passengers every time it docks.

Venice received over six hundred passenger ships last year and nearly six hundred monster ferries. Sometimes they arrive at the rate of ten a day.

And it's destroying the very thing they all came to see—the city of Venice. Water pollution, noise—the very vibrations of the giant ships rattle the ancient windows and shake the already shaky foundations.

An Italian heritage group reckons that Venice is already handling more than twice the number of visitors it can sustain, with no end in sight. What has been called the most beautiful city ever built is choking to death. It's not the City of Bridges or the City of Canals. It's Disneyland with Pasta.

And the Gulf Islands in the middle of a sea of twenty million residents with millions of tourists streaming in and out every year? Disneyland with Doug fir, maybe. Unless they needed to clear-cut for more parking.

I don't think it's a place I'd want to visit. And I damn sure wouldn't want to live there.

Everything New Is Old Again

If we could time travel back and stand at the head of Salt Spring's main harbour, around the year 1916, we'd be looking at the future site of the town of Ganges. Already there's a fair clustering of folks here: maybe a hundred settlers of European extraction; some Kanakas from the Hawaiian Islands; a few black refugees from the slave states to the south; and some been-here-forever Cowichan people shaking their heads and wondering where all the funny-looking strangers came from.

And those lights up there on the hill—that would be Harbour House, soon to become one of Salt Spring's fanciest hostelries. In 1916 it's just a guest house but eventually it will boast two of the best tennis courts in Canada, a salt-water swimming pool and on Sunday afternoons, parasols, white dresses and high tea on the front lawn. All this before the halfway mark of the last century. Not just a high-toned inn—a farm to boot. As a matter of fact Harbour House started out as a farm run by Fred Crofton, an Irish immigrant. He bought one hundred uncleared acres in 1904 and put most of it into cultivation. That's not all Fred and his wife, Nona, cultivated. By the 1930s the place was overrun by the seven Ds. Fred and Nona had a thing about the fourth letter of the alphabet and it showed in the names of their kids: Desmond, Dermot, Donovan, Dulcie, Doreen, Denise and Diana.

And what a farm those Croftons ran. They grew fruits and

vegetables and raised cattle, swine and poultry. More than enough to supply the hotel and a good bit of the populace.

And then, sometime around the mid-1950s, something happened. The world changed. Thanks to refrigeration and storage and cheap transportation, it became—illogically—cheaper to import food from the Okanagan, Washington and California than it was to grow it locally. Bit by bit Harbour House sold off its livestock and poultry.

Wild broom crept into the wheat fields and vegetable patches. The Harbour House farm went fallow. It stayed that way for more than half a century.

I don't know if there was any direct connection but Harbour House itself kind of went fallow too. It actually burned down a couple of times, and during one of its resurrections back in the '60s and '70s it got a little . . . rough around the edges. As a local observer put it: Harbour House went from high tea to rock 'n' roll. Somebody else said, back then if it was Saturday night and you were looking for a good fight, Harbour House was the place to be.

Well, the good news? Harbour House—the genteel version—is back. The better news? So is the farm. Right behind the hotel—and visitors are welcome to stroll through it—you'll find the new/old Harbour House farm. They've got greenhouses and outdoor raised beds, grain fields, beehives for honey and bigleaf maple trees for syrup—seventeen acres, all organic. And all patrolled by hot and cold running goats. Those goats aren't for meat or milk—they get a free ride because they actually eat broom, blackberry vines and thistles.

Belinda Schroeder is the person in charge of the Harbour House farm. She's an organic purist who'd sooner roll naked in a patch of stinging nettle than allow an ounce of herbicide or pesticide on her land. The food she grows there is as pure as food gets. And her primary customers? Guests at the Harbour House Hotel. She says she has no problem delivering thirty pounds of potatoes a day, plus all the fruits and vegetables the hotel can use.

So, in an age of financial instability, economic uncertainty and agricultural dubiousness, a smidgen of good news. A small hotel on a small island that was food self-sufficient nearly a hundred years ago is on its way to being self-sufficient again. The Crofton family doesn't own it anymore, but Jack Woodward, who took it over about five years ago, said at the time, "I think what Salt Spring needs is some continuity."

I'd say Salt Spring's got some. And I'm sure that Fred and Nona Crofton, not to mention Desmond, Dermot, Donovan, Dulcie, Doreen, Denise and Diana—would be pleased.

PART FIVE

Closed Captioned
for the Language Impaired

Parlez-Vous "Cop"?

If there's one thing that separates police officers from the rest of us—aside from the fact that he or she wears a gun and can seriously interfere with the way the rest of your day plays out—it's the way they talk. Particularly when they talk for publication. If, for instance, you or I came across a burglary in progress, we would relate the story something like, "Yeah, I was coming home from lunch when I saw this drunk smash through the glass door at the jewellery shop. The cops came along, he tried to run, they tackled him, cuffed him and read him his rights."

But the official description would be more like, "The suspect was observed entering the aforementioned premises at or about 1300 hours Greenwich Mean Time. Subject was observed to be in possession of a metal lever-like device, which was used to effect entry and subsequently brandished in a threatening manner. Officers on the scene exited the patrol vehicle and apprehended the perpetrator in order to neutralize the situation and secure the premises . . ." etcetera, etcetera.

It's classic cop-speak. I don't know why they do it, but it's weird and sometimes it's next to unintelligible. And I'm glad to see that some of our local cops are actually swimming against the Blue Tide. Cop reports with a dash of wit in them—who'da thunk it?

It's coming out of the Saanich Police Department on Vancouver Island in the form of otherwise boring and forgettable crime bulletins. Sergeant Dean Janzen is the public information officer for the Saanich department, and his motive, aside from making a dull chore more interesting, is pretty straightforward. "If you inject a little humour in police reports, you stand a far better chance of the message being carried further."

What kind of messages? Well, there's the case of the Chip Bandits. A woman in Victoria was awakened by her growling Chihuahua (hey, would I make this up?), which alerted her to the fact that there were prowlers in her attached garage. The police came, investigated and asked what if anything was missing. "My barbecue-flavoured chips," harrumphed the woman. A brief search of the neighbourhood turned up a pair of skunk-drunk women sprawled on a lawn munching on— uh-huh! Book 'em, Danno—a bag of barbecue-flavoured chips. The official police report concludes: "It appears the effervescent chips seen shimmering in the moonlight were too yummy to pass up when you have the munchies." Unquote.

Sometimes the titles of the police reports alone sound like episodes of a sitcom in progress. "A Mister Bean Style Robbery," reads one; "The Curious Case of the Constantly Stolen Truck," reads another. And my overall favourite: the report regarding a "man with a gun" incident that the Saanich Emergency Task Force responded to a few weeks back. No shots were fired. No blood was shed. The suspect had in fact a curling iron in his pants. The Saanich police report carried the deadpan heading "Dangerous Hair Styling Incident."

Some old-school law enforcement types no doubt frown upon Sergeant Janzen and his droll approach to crime reporting, but I think it's a breath of fresh air. And I look forward to his assessment of the recent theft of two Porta Potties that used to sit in the Saanich Police Department parking lot. I imagine it will read, "Thieves broke into the local police compound and stole two toilets. Police say they have nothing to go on."

It's all right, officer. I'll come quietly.

English as She Is Spoke

If the English language made any sense "lackadaisical"
would have something to do with a shortage of flowers.
—DOUG LARSON

But it doesn't—make any sense, I mean. Why, for instance, would any decent tongue adorn itself with contronyms? These are words that, depending on context, can mean the exact opposite of what they seem to mean. Thus, we have the word "cleave," which can mean to stick together or to rend asunder. We have "fast," which can mean speedy—or utterly immobile. A trip to Gay Paree is not the same as a trip over a loose shoelace. The alarm on your bedside clock goes off by going on. A pyromaniac/author could put out a fire—or put out a new book (*Fifty Shades of Black*, D&M, 256 pages).

And if that author was a sado-masochistic opportunist he could flog himself—or his book (Fifty Shades of Black, D&M, 256 pages).

Don't panic—I'm about to wind up this contronym tangent I'm on. But do I mean wind up as in "bring to an end"—or wind up as with a baseball pitch?

Forget contronyms, what about verbing? Your English teacher might call it "the practice of denominalizing—turning nouns into verbs." I call it a viral plague. Much of it is computer-based. "Blog" is a word that isn't even old enough to vote—it's derived from "web log" and has led to bloggers, blogging, even blogosphere. Hideous words all, but like warts on a toad, with us for the duration. Likewise "google," formerly a noun (google it, if you don't believe me); also xerox, fax and text.

There's nothing wrong with turning nouns into verbs; it goes on all the time. One can dress in a dress, dream a dream and dance a dance, but where do you draw the line?

For me, it's at Facebook. I won't join the social phenomenon because I cringe at the thought of "friending" anyone. It just sounds creepy and vaguely pedophilic. And unfriending????? Puh-leeeze.

I am much more amenable to the idea of paraprosdokians. A paraprosdokian is a figure of speech in which the latter part of a sentence or phrase is surprising or unexpected. The best one I ever heard sprang from the lips of John Wilkes, an English politician who was lambasted by the Earl of Sandwich a couple of centuries ago. The earl roared at him in the House of Commons, "I do not know, sir, if you will die on the gallows or of the pox" (i.e., of syphilis). Quick as a flash Wilkes stood up and purred, "That depends, my Lord, on whether I embrace your Lordship's principles, or your mistress."

Paraprosdokians don't have to be that exquisitely elaborate. Dorothy Parker was a master (mistress?) of the genre. She once sniffed, "I know a woman who speaks eighteen languages and can't say 'No' in any of them." Another time: "I require only three things of a man: he must be handsome, ruthless and stupid."

But the master of paraprosdokians? Sir Winston, of course. Churchill once explained his facility with English. It sprang, he said, from his poor scholarship. Other students were taught Latin and Greek but because he was considered "slow" he was taught only English. "As I remained [in third year] three times as long as anyone else, I had three times as much of it. I learned it thoroughly. Thus I got into my bones the essential structure of the English sentence—which is a noble thing."

It certainly was when filtered through the Churchillian vocal cords.

Such as the occasion when a moustachioed young Winston was confronted by an angry female voter. "Young man," she sniffed, "I care for neither your politics nor your moustache."

"Madam," responded Churchill, "you are unlikely to come into contact with either."

S'up with English? LOL!

Perhaps of all the creations of man, language is the most astonishing.

—Lytton Strachey

What do you suppose man's first word was? Not much more than a grunt, I reckon—post-prandial or post-coital most likely, acknowledging a full belly or satisfying sex. What a wonder that we could evolve from such a scattering of glottal oinks and ughs to a world that, according to the Ethnologue (www.ethnologue.com), currently features 6,912 tongues spoken by somebody somewhere on the earth's surface. Eighty-six of those languages are spoken here in Canada. They range from the Afrikaans of South African immigrants to Xaad Kil of our longest-standing citizens on Haida Gwaii.

And of course, there's English. About 375 million earthlings speak it as their first language but its true power is revealed in those who claim it as linguistic backup. Non-native English speakers outnumber the rest of us by about three to one. Which country do you think has the most people who speak or understand English? Great Britain? The US?

Nope—it's India. Not surprising when you realize that English is the tongue of choice in international diplomacy, medicine, communications, science, aviation and show biz.

And if you're a native English speaker as I am, let us go down on our knees together and thank providence for our lucky birthright, because learning to speak English as a second language must be a certifiable nightmare.

Are you kidding? A language in which you fill in a form by filling it out? Your house burns up as it burns down? Wristwatches run but time flies? You tell people you couldn't care less by saying, "I could care less"?

We've got ourselves a language that says it's perfectly permissible to drive on a parkway but park in a driveway. Our alarm clocks go off by going on, when the stars come out we can see them, but when the lights go out we can't see anything.

English is also the queen of oxymorons. It permits us to watch "awfully good" "half-naked" "light-heavyweights" pummel each other in rings that are square.

You are allowed, in English, to put your best foot forward while keeping your nose to the grindstone, your shoulder to the wheel, your eye on the ball and your tongue in cheek behind your stiff upper lip.

Not to mention knuckling down with your nose in the air, your chin up and your feet on the ground while head over heels.

Unless, of course, you don't have the stomach for it.

The adjectival form of "quiz" is quizzical.

So the adjectival form of "test" would be . . . ?

And what's with the word "haemorrhoid"?

Surely that should be "asteroid."

English is a language designed to torment and befuddle. Imagine trying to teach a non-English speaker how to pronounce "ough."

It's an "oo" sound, of course—as in "through."

Or is it an "uff" sound—as in "tough"?

Or an "ow" sound—as in "plough"?

That's only the beginning. Here's a phrase we can all be proud of: Boughs brought nought through—thought enough?

And don't forget the "up" sound of "hiccough."

It may be slight consolation that at least one expert thinks traditional spelling—indeed, pretty well all spelling—is on the way out, thanks to the Internet. David Crystal, a linguistics professor at the University of Wales, points out that for the first time in many hundreds of years, much of the printed word is being distributed without benefit of editors or proofreaders. Bloggers blog, texters text and, dare I say, twits tweet—all without any Higher Power correcting or rewriting their efforts. Short forms abound. "By the way" becomes BTW; IMHO stands in for "in my humble opinion."

Professor Crystal claims to be unfazed by this development. "The vast majority of spelling rules in English are irrelevant," says the prof breezily.

All I can say is: WTF? Itz all 2 depressing 4 me.

C U L8TR.

If It's Okay with You . . .

I'd like to write a few lines about a tiny word that is the very glue of the English language, okay? Now, it's entirely okay if you're not personally okay with that, but I got the okay from my editor. Usually she shrugs when I suggest a theme and offers a grudging "okay. "But this time she really liked it. "O-KAY!" she said. "Go for it!"

Versatile little four-letter combination when you think about it—especially when you realize it can be cut in half and still say the same thing. My dictionary recognizes "O.K." and even "OK" as legitimate variations. They all sound exactly the same to the human ear.

"Okay" is probably the best-known English word in the world. Venetian gondoliers get "okay"; so do Tibetan Sherpas, Australian outbackers, Colombian drug mules and Chinese moneylenders.

So where does okay come from?

How much time have you got?

Over the years linguists have proposed that the expression was swiped from the Scots (*och aye*), West African slaves (*wah kay*), the French (*au quais*), the Choctaw tribe (*o keh*), the Finns (*oikea*)—even from a US railway freight agent named Obadiah Kelly who was in the habit of scrawling his initials as a signature on bills of lading.

The only thing pretty much everyone agreed on is that usage as an English expression bubbled up in eastern North America sometime in the early nineteenth century.

By 1840, rumours attributed the phrase to US president Andrew

Jackson. Detractors said that President Jackson scrawled O.K. on government documents under the illusion he was using a short form for "all correct." (Orl Korect?)

Cute story, but highly unlikely. Andrew Jackson was a well-educated man.

Whatever the origins, "okay" was perfectly okay to use through North America by the 1850s—so much so that it appears in the written works of Henry David Thoreau in 1854. Now, a century and a half later, the word has been bisected again. People often signify acceptance with a single syllable instead of two.

"You wanna grab a bite at the Taco Bell?"

"Kay."

Fortunately, thanks to the work of a US professor named Allen Walker Read, we now know the true origins of this ubiquitous phrase. Professor Read figured it out by poring over back issues of eastern American newspapers published in the early to mid-1800s.

Turns out there was a kind of fad that swept the chattering classes of early nineteenth-century Boston society, in which people wishing to appear clever used abbreviations to replace well-known phrases. Thus, people would say (or write) ISBD instead of It Shall Be Done. Boston's leading citizens were referred to as OFMs—Our First Men. And anything insignificant was dismissed with SP—Small Potatoes.

Another craze those early language manglers indulged in was faux illiteracy. They liked to pretend they couldn't spell very well. Thus the Boston aristocracy (Andrew Jackson had nothing to do with it) brutalized the phrase "all correct" into "orl correct"—which got shortened to O.K.

And the rest is history, okay?

Using Phroper English

I love this job. It may not pay much but it's full of surprises. Yesterday I rambled into my favourite coffee shop and was instantly accosted by one of the regulars. "Hey, Black!" he said by way of introduction. "You called" (insert Member of Parliament's name here) "a 'nimrod' in your column last week. You know what a nimrod is?"

A nimrod, I replied, is a fool, a klutz, an idiot, a clown. You think I was too kind?

"Hah!" said my inquisitor. "You're dead wrong! A nimrod is a mighty hunter!"

Well, literally and technically, yeah. "Nimrod," according to the Bible, was a great-grandson of Noah. He became a king and founded Babylon. He was also, legend has it, a guy who knew his way around a bow and arrow, a spear, a dagger and other instruments of interspecies domination.

"Nimrod" ought to reflect that heady lineage and be a word of praise but it's not. It means, in fact, precisely the opposite. If somebody calls you a nimrod, they are probably Not Your Friend.

Elmer Fudd—especially when he's duded out in a deerstalking cap, his Eddie Bauer hunting vest and toting a shotgun through the bush, fruitlessly flailing the bushes in search of Bugs Bunny—is a nimrod.

So what do you call a word or a phrase that actually means the opposite of what it's supposed to mean? You call it a "phrop." A fascinating chap by the name of Sir Arnold Lunn (mountaineer, world-class skier and amateur wordsmith) made up the word by combining "phrase" and "opposite" and lopping their tails off, nimrod-style.

We use phrops from time to time—at least I know I do. When I say to the annoying lapel-clinger who's been dogging me at a party, "We must do lunch one day," what I really mean is, "If I can help it, this is the last time in recorded history that we will be in one another's presence, unless we have the misfortune to share a common graveyard." Similarly, when someone launches into a critique of something I've written with the words, "With all due respect," I know that I'm about to be linguistically cross-checked, head-butted, rabbit-punched and groin-kneed and "due respect" will not be much in evidence.

Canadians resilient and adventurous enough to watch the cable TV public affairs channel CPAC may happen upon *Question Period* from the House of Commons in Ottawa. There they will see phrops flying back and forth like badminton birdies. A reference to a challenge from "my learned colleague" sitting across the floor really means, "I can't believe I have to waste my time responding to this pompous gasbag." And when Stephen Harper addresses Thomas Mulcair as "the Right Honourable Leader of the Opposition," his tone, his body language and those rattlesnake eyes portend a classic phrop in the making.

Canadian politicians, alas, are not in the same league as a silver-tongued phropist like the nineteenth-century British prime minister Benjamin Disraeli, who wrote to a novelist seeking his endorsement, "Thank you for sending me your book. I shall waste no time reading it."

But you don't have to go to the House of Commons, British or Canadian, to hear a decent phrop.

When someone butts in front of you with, "I hope you don't mind ..." he doesn't really give a bleep what you think.

When someone says, "I don't wanna brag, but . . . " he's about to brag.

When someone says, "To be perfectly frank . . . " she's about to lie.

When someone says, "I'm telling you this for your own good . . ." (see "With all due respect" above).

But a phrop is not always a weaselly linguistic manoeuvre. Sometimes it's so perfect that it's sublime. A few years ago, an Oxford language philosopher by the name of J.L. Austin was lecturing a class on the phenomenon of double negatives—when two "no" words are used in the same clause. He told his listeners that many languages use double negatives to make a positive but double positives are never, ever used to make a negative.

From the back of the class came a muttered, "Yeah. Right."

Words at Work

If the English language made any sense "fish and chips" might be spelled "ghoti and tchoghs." (Fish: "gh" as in rough, "o" as in women, "ti" as in ration. Chips: "tch" as in catch, "o" as in women, "gh" as in hiccough.) If English made any sense there would not be eight different ways to pronounce the letter sequence "ough" (through, thought, though, cough, rough, bough, thorough—and don't forget hiccough).

But English, bless 'er, seldom makes sense. Our language is like a rogue blue whale on a methamphetamine run, thrashing through the Sea of Tongues gobbling up choice morsels left and right while wreaking tail-smacking havoc on other etymologies. As the Canadian writer James Nicoll says, "English is about as pure as a cribhouse whore. We don't just borrow words; on occasion, English has pursued other languages down alleyways to beat them unconscious and rifle their pockets for new vocabulary."

That's how we picked up algebra (Arabic), skeleton (Greek), grotesque (Italian), mosquito (Spanish), keelhaul (Dutch), pyjamas (Urdu), zombie (West African), ski (Norwegian), blitzkrieg (German) and potlatch (Nuu-chah-nulth)—just to name a handful.

But we don't just steal words, we invent new ones all the time. Some words that gained official status in the *Oxford English Dictionary* recently include: wonky, WiFi, looky-loo and low-rent. Some words the OED honchos tossed over the side to make room for the newcomers:

abstergent (cleansing), caducity (perishableness) and griseous (streaked with grey).

I won't miss those words (mainly because I never knew they existed) but the authorities also deep-sixed a number of worthies that I think still have plenty of tread on their tires. What's wrong with "embrangle" (to confuse or entangle)? Why are we ditching a splendid word like "niddering" (cowardly)? And isn't "fubsy" (short and stout, squat) just too good to kill? A malison (curse) upon the heads of the butchers who excised these words from our lexicon. And yes, "malison" is also on the chopping block.

Speaking of chopping block, the British Sociological Association, an umbrella group for many professors, lecturers, researchers and other sundry British academics, has announced that its members will henceforth be enjoined from using the term "Old Masters" when referring to, er, Old Masters. Why? Too sexist, old chap. What about all those Old Mistresses, eh wot? The BSA (ironic abbreviation, that) is also banning the "racist" words "immigrant," "developing nations" and—I'm not pulling your leg—"black."

I guess name-wise, the BSA has left me SOL.

Not to worry. I consider the English tongue to be—at the risk of being slammed for sexism—a feisty old broad who's outmanoeuvred tougher foes than the British Sociological Association.

She has to be tough—look at the idiots who abuse her. From monosyllabic teenagers who can't string a thought sequence together without slapping on bandages and twist ties like "awesome" and, well, "like" . . .

"So she wuz like, 'You know that dude? Awesome!' An' I wuz, like, 'Whatever.'"

. . . to Bureaucratese. How would a civil servant suggest that someone might be lying? Here's how Sir Humphrey Appleby did it in *Yes, Minister*:

"Sometimes one is forced to consider the possibility that affairs are being conducted in a manner which, all things being considered and making all possible allowances is, not to put to fine a point on it, perhaps not entirely straightforward."

Words, all words. "Words are like loaded pistols," according to Jean-Paul Sartre. Rudyard Kipling called them "the most powerful drug used by mankind."

More than eight centuries ago a Zen master named Dai-O Kokushi explained words in a koan:

> Wishing to entice the blind,
> The Buddha playfully let words escape from his golden mouth;
> Heaven and earth are filled, ever since, with entangling briars.

Or, as George Carlin put it: "I don't have to tell you it goes without saying there are some things better left unsaid. I think that speaks for itself. The less said about it the better."

Name That Town

When it came to slapping names on chunks of this country our forefathers (and mothers) were a relatively adventurous lot. They tapped royalty (Victoria, Regina, Alberta), explorers (Vancouver, Hudson), local topography (Montreal, after Mount Royal), forgettable politicians (Kitchener, Hamilton) and saints (Sault Ste. Marie, St. Catharines, St. John and just in case we missed the point, St. John's).

Occasionally they aped their betters (London, Warsaw, Paris, Berlin—all in Ontario); other times they realized they couldn't improve on the originals and simply stole the First Nations names already in place: Saskatoon, Winnipeg, Toronto, Mississauga.

Eclectic and wide-ranging—not a dull or boring name in the lot.

Not like, well, Dull and Boring. You'll find the former in Scotland and the latter in Oregon. Dull (population eighty-four) is a tiny village in Perthshire; Boring is a not-so-tiny burg of ten thousand or so Oregonians located about twenty miles south of Portland.

Ironic when you think about it. We Canadians are the ones with the rep for being dull and boring, but you wouldn't know it by the names of our towns and cities. As a matter of fact, a visitor might get the impression Canucks are downright colourful—and unabashedly randy.

From the Far North (Steambath Lake, Yukon; Hump Island, NWT) to the Deep South (Middlesex, Ontario), Canada has a steamy sheet of place names that would make Madonna blush.

British Columbia has a Sin Lake, Moan Creek, Shag Rock and Peekaboo Falls. Alberta can claim Sexsmith and Spanking Lake. Saskatchewan? Well, there's Lust Lake and Climax, for starters. Manitoba gives us Love Lake, Cuddle Bay and Strip Rapids.

In Ontario there's Flesherton, Bottomlands and Peeler Lake.

And Quebec? *Quelle surprise.* La Belle Province teems with suggestive nomenclature—Lac Brassière, Lac de la Caresse, Lac Eros and even Lac Latex.

Plus—gasp!—the Gaspé Peninsula.

The Maritimes won't be left behind in the erotic topography department—not while there's a Kissing Brook or a Lover's Cove to be found on your GPS.

And then there's Newfoundland. Even if the entire upper two-thirds of the North American continent was as dull and boring as, well, Dull and Boring, we'd still have Canada's youngest province whistling and twirling its moustache, winking like the porch light on Hugh Hefner's pad.

Look at the names in that province! Never mind the obvious Dildo and Come By Chance—how about Bare Bum Pond? Naked Man? Leading Tickles? And my favourite: Pinch Gut Tickle.

I'm not sure if that's an S&M option or an illegal wrestling hold but it sounds way more intriguing than Lloydminster or Sydney.

Naming geographical entities is a tricky business; you want to be careful who gets the honour to take it on. There's a city named Å in Sweden and a bay named Y in the Zuider Zee. France has an island named If, a river named As and a lake named Oo.

On the other hand, there is a town in Wales that goes by the name of Llanfairpwllgwyngyllgogerychwyrndrobwllllantysiliogogogoch.

Some people think we'd avoid confusion and misunderstanding if citizens got to vote on the names of towns, rivers, public buildings, etc.

Don't bet on it.

Recently, a Slovakian government opened online voting to name a bridge over the Morava River. Seventy-five percent of the populace came up with the same choice.

And that's why the new span over the Morava River will be known to posterity as Chuck Norris Bridge.

Errors and That Typo Thing

*I was a good typist; at my high school typing was regarded
as a secondary female sex characteristic, like breasts.*
—MARGARET ATWOOD

I'm not surprised that Margaret Atwood was a good typist. She's
great at everything she does. Me? I'm a lousy typist (my breasts
are no hell either) but I don't fret about it because when it comes to
typing, Fate has given all of us, ept and otherwise, a great levelling
device.

The typo.

Anybody, saint or sinner, genius or journeyman, can make a typographical error. It's simply a mistake made in the typing of a document
or other printed material. Now, thanks to that infernal computer Nazi
called spell-check, typos are even easier to make.

Yew sea wad eye mien, daunt ewe?

Typos are usually meaningless but occasionally hilarious. Not long
ago the *Toronto Sun* ran a short item apologizing for an error. "Incorrect
information appeared in a column," the piece began. Unfortunately it
ran under a boldface headline that read "CORRERCTION."

A college catalogue description for a course in Shakespeare:
"Intensive analysis of Hamlet, Macbeth and Anatomy and Cleopatra."

A luncheon menu: "Today's special: Dreaded Veal Cutlet."

And the *New York Post* is a two-time loser. On Monday it ran a
story that said: "Sergeant Alfred Blaine is a twenty-year defective on
the New York police force."

The next day it ran a correction: "Sergeant Alfred Blaine is a twenty-year detective on the New York Police Farce."

My favourite typo occurred nearly 150 years ago. It was made by a German chemist studying the iron content of vegetables. In transcribing data from his notebook, the chemist ascribed thirty-five milligrams of iron to each one hundred gram serving of spinach.

Big mistake. He should have put a decimal point between the three and the five, i.e., 3.5 milligrams per one hundred grams.

It was only a dot—the smallest typographical mark you can make—but it transformed a so-so green into a miracle muscle-builder and eventually gave us Popeye the Sailor Man:

> I'm strong to the finish
> 'Cuz I eats me spinach
> I'm Popeye the Sailor Man.

The popularity of the Popeye comic strip increased American consumption of spinach by over 30 percent.

So. If we had Truth in Advertising?

> Me muskels is hard
> 'Cuz I eats me chard.

Nah. Just doesn't sing.

The Not-So-Grand Ole Opry

I don't like country music, but I don't mean to denigrate those who do. And for the people who like country music, "denigrate" means "put down."

—Bob Newhart

I'm not quite as dismissive as Mr. Newhart is on the subject of country music. I have more of a love-loathe relationship with the genre. I love the simple honesty of a Hank Williams *père* tune, the stately grace of a Carter Family ballad and the intricacies of anything finger-picked by Doc Watson. I loathe the hokey, flag-waving, rhinestone cowboy maudlin crap into which so much country music has descended of late.

Maybe it's the artists. Perhaps it's the audiences. What has seventy-two legs and twenty-three teeth?

The front row of a Willie Nelson concert.

It's easy to make fun of country music because so much of it is excruciatingly bad but that doesn't mean it can't be taken seriously. Recently, a scientific paper appeared in the pages of the *Review of General Psychology*, the very title of which must have tweaked a few scholarly eyebrows. The paper was called "Cheatin' Hearts and Loaded Guns." It wasn't a smackdown of country music; it was a sober investigation of what those hurtin' songs really mean. According to Robert Kurzban, the paper's author, "Country music feeds our desire to learn about things that carry high fitness consequences in the world."

That's convoluted psychobabble that really means country songs are morality tales. They tell the listener what happens when you go off the straight and narrow. All those mournful yodellings about trucks and gals and bars and jails aren't really about trucks and gals and bars and jails, they're actually musical instruction booklets full of advice about human survival and sexual reproduction.

Sexual reproduction? You bet.

How about Loretta Lynn's "Don't Come Home a-Drinkin' (With Lovin' on Your Mind)"?

Survival? I give you "I Been Roped and Thrown by Jesus in the Holy Ghost Corral." Not to mention "Drop Kick Me Jesus, through the Goalposts of Life."

On a more secular plane, country songs address the eternal verities like Heartbreak: "I Got Tears in My Ears from Lying on My Bed Crying on My Pillow over You."

Or the even more magnificent Garth Brooks lyric from a ditty called "Papa Loved Mama": "Papa loved mama, mama loved men; mama's in the graveyard, papa's in the pen."

Alcohol looms large in country music. Witness the songs "80 Proof Bottle of Tear Stopper" and also "I Want a Beer Cold as My Ex-Wife's Heart."

Failed relationships are prominent too, as in George Strait's "All My Exes Live in Texas."

Occasionally a country song comes along that manages to turn a double play. Here's one that addresses gambling and heartbreak: "I Gave My Heart a Diamond and She Clubbed Me with a Spade."

Personally, I prefer the simpler titles such as "Bubba Shot the Jukebox" and also "Velcro Arms, Teflon Heart"—but I've always been an incurable romantic.

It's a macho world, is country music, but some of its biggest stars are women and female sensibilities are beginning to make inroads. A singer by the name of Miranda Lambert croons a vengeful little ballad that includes these lines: "Slapped my face and he shook me like a rag doll. Don't that sound like a real man? I'm gonna show him what a little girl's made of. Gunpowder and lead."

A little too John Wayne–ish for me. I prefer the caustic wit of Deana Carter's song "Did I Shave My Legs for This?"

Professor Kurzban, the man behind the paper "Cheatin' Hearts and Loaded Guns," insists country music survives because it "satisfies an informational need." Well, maybe—but it's funnybone fodder too. Hard to improve on a title like "Walk Out Backwards So I'll Think You're Walking In."

Cole Porter, eat your heart out.

You know what happens if you play a country music song backwards, don't you? Your girlfriend returns, your pickup is un-repossessed, your hangover disappears, your dog comes back to life and you get a pardon from the warden.

Shoo Fly, Don't Bother Me

I am walking in the woods with my dogs. I am peaceful. Centred. At one with the Great Green Goddess. I spy another couple walking down the path. I know them slightly and we pause to chat.

But something is amiss. We palaver amiably enough but they seem ill at ease, unwilling to meet my gaze. They look to the heavens; they study their shoelaces. They crane to the east and they peer to the west. They will not look me in the eye.

After several awkward moments we part company and I am left with my dogs to wonder—a forgotten slight? Something I wrote perhaps? A few hundred yards down the trail my hand brushes across my thighs and I solve the mystery.

Oh crap. My fly's open again.

I don't know if it's a harbinger of impending geezerdom or mere wishful thinking, but I find my fly seems to be at half-mast more often of late. Odd, when you consider that "doing up your fly" is something all lads are supposed to master before they get out of knee pants. Doubly odd, when you consider that a gaping fly is a no-win condition. Mortification all around.

Geoffrey Chaucer and his Middle Ages pals didn't have to worry about accidental breaches in their breeches. They wore codpieces—a kind of sliding manhole cover (think of it as a man bra but with only one cup).

Codpieces were functional but less than subtle, fashion-wise. Along about 1700, tailors came up with what they called a "fall front"—a flap of fabric that functioned something like the breechclout that North American Indians had figured our centuries before.

When you think about it mankind has never had a rock-solid solution for the codpiece/fall front/button/zip fly problem. What complicates the conundrum is that men are lazy slobs. We want to get 'er done with a minimum of interruption and inconvenience. Women don't have a fly problem because they sit down and do the job properly.

And obviously, women don't have an open fly problem either. If they did, they would doubtless have come up with a diplomatic, non-humiliating way to say, "Hey, buddy . . . your fly is open."

Not that there haven't been some splendid attempts. General euphemisms for informing someone that their clothing is in need of adjustment abound. I'm rather fond of "Paging Mr. Johnson . . . Paging Mr. Johnson . . ." I'm also intrigued with the idea of putting on a big black studly voice and rumbling, "I'm talkin' Shaft—can you dig it?"

"Security breach at Los Pantalones" isn't half-bad, nor is "Our next guest is someone who needs no introduction . . ." But personally, I prefer the individual touch—warnings custom-crafted for the poor schlub with the open portal problem.

For a dishevelled computer nerd: "Excuse me, but you have Windows on your laptop."

For vegetarians: "Don't look now but the cucumber has left the salad."

For rock fans: "Attention, attention . . . Elvis Junior has left the building."

For nautical types: "Now hear this: Sailor Ned's trying to take a little shore leave."

For airline passengers with a fly problem: "Time to bring your tray table to the upright and locked position, sir."

For lovers of classical literature: "Quasimodo needs to go back in the tower and tend to his bells."

What's also missing is a suitable retort to the news that your fly is open. Usually it's a mumbled "Oh, geez, thanks eh?"

Pretty lame.

Winston Churchill knew how to handle such a situation. Using the facilities in the House of Commons one day during his final years in office, Winston turned from the urinal to the washstand, only to be confronted by a fellow MP who fluttered about trying to tell him the bad news as delicately as possible.

"Ah, Sir Winston, you should know . . . ah, that is to say, er. You . . . um . . . oh dear. It seems your flies are open."

"What of it?" growled the ninety-year-old Churchill. "Dead birds don't fall out of nests."

Best Job in the World

I've had a lot of jobs in my life, but I still remember my first one with great fondness. I started out as a newspaper editor.

The Editor's Chair is not usually offered to a greenhorn kid with no relevant experience but this was different—I owned the newspaper. I was also the Publisher, Advertising Manager and (lone) Feature Reporter.

I'm fairly certain the editorial departments of *The Globe and Mail* and the *Toronto Star* didn't lose a lot of sleep over the launching of my periodical. It only lasted for a single edition, peaking at a circulation of one. It consisted of one front page that featured a news flash hand-printed on kraft paper and accompanied by a (very bad) drawing of something with feathers. The headline: UNUSUAL BIRD SPOTTED ON MR. RUTHERFORD'S LAWN.

Well, whaddya expect? I was nine years old.

I didn't last long as an editor but that first bite of the newspaper bug proved highly infectious. In the years that followed I tried on a lot of different hats—farmhand, seaman, English teacher, salesman, actor, radio commentator, television show host . . .

And here I am again—back in the newspaper business. Only a columnist this time, nothing as exalted as the editorship, but still.

Mind you, I have a ways to go to fill the shoes of Newt Wallace of Winters, California. Newt's been in the newspaper business since 1947, and he operates at a journalistic level even more fundamental than writing or editing. Newt delivers copies of the *Winters Express* to customers on the same route he's trudged pretty well every publishing day for the past sixty-six years.

That's right, Newt Wallace is a paperboy—if you can call a ninety-three-year-old guy who delivers your paper a boy.

He was delivering papers even before that. He had his own route at the age of twelve back in Muskogee, Oklahoma. Then he did a stint in the navy, accumulated a bit of a bankroll, heard there was a small paper for sale way out in Winters, California, hopped a train to check it out and bought the *Winters Express*, lock, stock and printing press for $12,500 back in 1946. He ran the paper and delivered the copies until 1983 when his son took over. Wallace senior tried retirement, found it didn't fit and asked for his delivery job back.

"I don't hunt or play golf," Newt told a reporter. "I deliver papers."

Is he going to give it up now that he's heading for the century mark? Nope. "He tried to quit," his son recalls, "but I tell him, 'Show me three friends who are your age, retired and still alive.' He thinks about it and then he goes back to his desk."

The news business is like that—it gets in your blood.

If I ever grow up I'm going to apply for a paper route too.

PART SIX

Believe It or Not . . .

Mmm, Mmm! Cricket Cacciatore!

Are you a Chicken Marengo fancier? How about Steak Delmonico? Or (let's go über-gourmet) what do you say to a plate of Canard à la Rouennaise?

Sounds like you really like your meat. Well, savour it, you crazy carnivore, because your meat-eating days are numbered. It comes down to simple math. Global meat consumption in the developed world has doubled—let me say that again—doubled—since 1992. Meanwhile, the global population of meat-eating humans is jackrabbiting skyward every year. It all adds up to an unsustainable equation. Even McDonald's can't flip enough burgers to fill those gaping maws.

Which leaves us with, what—an unleavened future of bean burritos, lentil casseroles and Eggplant Zucchini Gratin?

Relax. The End of Meat does not mean we all have to become vegetarians. We haven't even begun to tap the biggest, infinitely sustainable, guilt-free source of protein on the planet.

Bugs.

No, wait—don't turn that page. It's true that we North American pantywaists find the idea of eating bugs repugnant, but we're a little behind the terrestrial curve on this one. Almost 80 percent of the world's population enthusiastically ingests insects on a regular basis. In East Africa, the midge fly is a delicacy. In Japan, even the emperor Hirohito was a big fan of boiled wasps with rice. They eat fried silkworms in Korea, Cambodian men turn to crispy tarantulas for a shot of natural Viagra and in movie theatres in Colombia you can buy a bag of fried leafcutter ants (their Spanish name means, literally, "big-ass ants") in place of the usual popcorn. The edible insect menu is endless and varied. On a recent trip to Thailand and Vietnam, I passed sidewalk stalls offering all manner of creepy-crawly taste delights including scorpions on a skewer.

And why not? Insects are high in protein, low in fat and cholesterol and a ready source of vitamins and minerals. Plus, you don't need a five hundred acre ranch or a two-storey pig barn to raise grasshoppers or crickets. I've got a decent free-range herd of the critters in my backyard.

You think eating bugs is sacrilegious? Guess again, Pilgrim:

"Even these of them ye may eat: the locust after its kind, and the bald locust after its kind, and the cricket after its kind, and the grasshopper after its kind."

Leviticus 11:22.

Here's the kicker: don't worry about adding insects to your diet—they're already there. An Ohio University study says we each, unknowingly, eat one to two pounds of insects every year.

It comes in our food, processed and unprocessed, and thanks to our agricultural practices it's unavoidable.

But is it dangerous to our health? *Au contraire.*

"They're actually pretty healthy," says Dr. Philip Nixon, an entomologist at the University of Illinois. "If we were more willing to accept certain defect levels such as insects and insect parts, growers could reduce pesticide usage. Some of the spraying that goes on is directly related to the aesthetics of our food."

Don't know about you, but I'm sold. *Bon appétit* and pass the crickets!

I don't know whether to start with a wing or a leg.

Tainted Money

You planning to spend any time in Vietnam or Thailand? Here's a hint: don't take travellers' cheques. They are next to worthless. In fact, unless you're looking for kindling to start a fire they ARE worthless. I spent an entire morning in Ho Chi Minh City last year going from bank to hotel to money-changer trying to cash an American Express traveller's cheque for a hundred dollars. They treated me like I was trying to palm off some satanic manifesto about the perfidies of Uncle Ho. Peeved, I unfolded my emergency fifty dollar US bill that I kept hidden behind my driver's licence and handed it to the teller at the last bank I tried. The teller took it suspiciously, squinted at it, then handed it back with a shake of her head.

What? They don't take American currency? When I persisted, she pointed to a check mark someone had made with a ballpoint pen right next to President Grant's portrait.

"Not take," she said firmly. "Dirty money."

Turns out that Asian banks—the ones I tried to deal with anyway— will only accept bills that are as unsullied and pristine as an Anne Murray lullaby. Corner missing? Sorry. Greasy, grimy or all crumpled up from being jammed in your sock? Too bad.

Weird. I've exchanged bills in Canadian banks that were so battered and mangled you couldn't tell if the lady on the front was Queen Elizabeth or Granny Clampett. As long as the serial numbers were intact, those bills were accepted without question.

But . . . perhaps not so weird. Scientists have been putting currency under the microscope recently and it turns out that our money really is dirty. Sometimes spectacularly so.

In a study published in the *Southern Medical Journal* experts pulled sixty-eight US one-dollar bills out of public circulation and tested them for contamination. A total of 94 percent of them failed to pass the test. True, most of them were merely crawling with "friendly" bacteria not dangerous to human health, but nearly 10 percent harboured potentially fatal pathogens including pneumonia, staphylococcus and the fecal bacteria E. coli.

And then there's the cocaine factor. In 2009 a study conducted by the University of Massachusetts tested over two hundred bills of various denominations collected from eighteen US cities. Some 90 percent of them showed traces of cocaine. Clearly, the ability of money to serve as a delivery system for unwanted substances is beyond doubt.

Makes sense when you think about it. Paper money sees a lot of life as it gets passed around through the sweaty hands of taxi drivers, bartenders, convenience store operators . . . who knows who's handled the money in your wallet? Who can tell if some of those bills you accept from the nice lady at the flower shop have been seeing active duty as a straw up some cokehead's nose or as a gratuity stuffed down a stripper's G-string?

Mind you, the odds in favour of clean (well, clean-ish) are better here in Canada. We don't have scuzzy one-dollar—or even two-dollar—bills in circulation anymore. We've replaced them with cold metal loonies and toonies that are much less hospitable to bacteria and viruses.

As for paper money, we've gotten rid of that, too. Our new bills are made of polymer, not paper. Not only are they harder to counterfeit, they're much more difficult to contaminate. Plastic is a poor host for those microscopic nasty critters that thrive on old-fashioned currency.

Mind you, those new Canadian bills may not be totally bug-free. A bank teller in Kelowna claims she's heard of an instance where several new hundred-dollar bills left in a car on a sweltering August afternoon melted and fused together.

Try cashing a blob of polymer at any bank—Vietnamese or Canadian.

Dirty money. Gives a whole new interpretation to the term "money laundering."

Mark Twain and an acquaintance were once shooting the breeze and the topic turned to a very rich man they both knew.

"Of course," the acquaintance sniffed, "his money is tainted."

"Yep," said Twain. "T'ain't yours and t'ain't mine."

A Sign of the Times

*There are limits to man's wisdom, but no limits on his
stupidity—and that's just not fair.*

—Konrad Adenauer

Sometimes I despair of our courts. One guy draws six months in
the slammer for knocking over a convenience store for chump
change; meanwhile British Columbia chiseller Ian Thow, who bilked
pensioners and small-time investors out of millions of dollars, gets a
powder-puff pat on the wrist and may well be back on the street by the
time you read this.

"The law," Charles Dickens has one of his characters opine, "is an
ass . . . an idiot."

Often true—but not always. Consider the case of the judge
in Cleveland, Ohio, who pronounced judgment on Shena Hardin
recently. Ms. Hardin had been caught on camera driving her car up on
a sidewalk to get around a school bus that was discharging children.
Her sentence? Neither fine nor jail time. She merely has to stand at a
major intersection for two school days wearing a sign around her neck
that says: ONLY AN IDIOT WOULD DRIVE ON THE SIDEWALK
TO AVOID A SCHOOL BUS.

As a punishment, that has a nice ring to it. As a matter of fact it has
a kind of universality that might well lend itself to other cases.

Republican congressman Paul Broun of Georgia, for example.
Congressman Broun recently cast doubt on the theories of evolution,
embryology and the big bang theory, dismissing them as "lies from the

pit of hell." The earth is only nine thousand years old, the congressman assured anyone who would listen, and anyone who disagreed with him was consigned to everlasting damnation.

It is somewhat dismaying to learn that Congressman Broun is a member of the US House Committee on Science, Space and Technology, but I think that would be negated nicely if he was required to wear a sign around his neck saying: I AM AN IDIOT.

And although he's no longer in a position to wear the sign, Edward Archibald of West Palm Beach would certainly qualify on behavioural grounds. Mr. Archibald recently won a bug-eating contest in his hometown by cramming wriggling worms, chirping crickets and live, three- to four-inch-long cockroaches into his mouth and swallowing them faster than any of the other twenty-nine contestants.

Alas, Mr. Archibald didn't get to enjoy first prize (a live python); he collapsed and died right after downing his last insect.

Although Mr. Archibald can't wear the sign around his neck, perhaps a placard declaring HE WAS AN IDIOT could be propped against his tombstone.

Idiot signs—it's a growth industry when you think about it. Consider: this past Halloween, Americans spent $370 million on Halloween costumes—for their pets. *Time* magazine says 15 percent of the population shelled out serious money to outfit their Chihuahuas and tortoiseshells in costumes ranging from Batman to Lady Gaga— that's forty-five million more idiot signs right there!

And as long as we're handing out awards how about a Lifetime Achievement I'M STILL AN IDIOT sign for Donald Trump? The bouffant-ed blowhard buffoon outdid himself during the last presidential election campaign, texting and tweeting paranoid and delusional denunciations of the US president. NBC anchorman Brian Williams nicely encapsulated the New York nutbar's contributions, saying that Trump had "driven well past the last exit to relevance and veered into something closer to irresponsible." Trump, meanwhile, was punching out tweets such as "Let's fight like hell and stop this great and disgusting injustice! The world is laughing at us!"

No, Donald. Only at you.

But we need to save one sign for a radio listener named Donna— mercifully we don't know her last name—who recently phoned up a radio open-line show in North Dakota to complain about the placement of "Deer Crossing" signs on busy roads.

Donna felt that the signs were hazardous and that the deer should be directed to cross roads in less travelled areas.

The radio show host assured her that actually . . . the signs weren't meant for the deer to read.

"I feel so stupid," said Donna. "I had no clue that these signs were for us."

Bubble-Wrap the Kiddies

In the first place, God made idiots. That was for practice.
Then he made school boards.

MARK TWAIN

News alert, folks—the Department of Education has just announced a ban on Christmas trees in schools. "Too many prickles," a spokesman said. "A child could choke on a pine or spruce needle and possibly die."

Nah, I'm joshing ya—but only just. Big Nurse is on the loose and she's determined to protect the little ones, even if it means you go to jail.

Ask the ladies who were enjoying doughnuts and coffee on a bench in one of New York City's public playgrounds last spring. Busted! The cops who gave them tickets also took down a notorious ring of seven senior male citizens operating inside the confines of yet another city playground. Their offence? Playing chess. Adults in New York are forbidden to even enter public playgrounds unless accompanied by a child.

Might be pedophiles, you know.

Several American libraries have caught the paranoia bug, banning unaccompanied adults from entering the children's book sections. There's one library in Pennsylvania that bans adults from using the restrooms "unless accompanied by their children."

So it's verboten for a solo grandpa to go to the john but it's okay for a pedophile to take a kid in with him? I'm confused.

It's just as dopey on this side of the border. Last summer a bunch of teenagers got together to play a game of pickup baseball on the grounds of Eagle View Elementary School in Victoria, BC. Why not? It was summertime, there were no classes being held, the field was empty. That's when the bylaw officer came over and asked them if they had a permit. They didn't. He kicked them off the property.

Just how safe do we want our kids to be? Bubble-wrap safe. Parents of children attending an elementary school in North Brookfield, Massachusetts, recently received a letter informing them that henceforth students were not to bring pens or pencils onto school property in pockets, binders or backpacks. Writing utensils would be handed out by school officials, as necessary. Sixth-grade teacher Wendy Scott went on to say that if any student was caught with a pen or pencil, he or she would be assumed to have stolen it from school with the intent "to build weapons."

Not that school kids need dangerous armament-building material like pencils and ballpoints to wreak havoc and destroy society as we know it. Alert teachers at a junior school in Bridlington, England, have ordered their students to stop raising their hands to answer questions. Head teacher Cheryl Adams explains that the tradition of hand-raising to respond to questions "creates too much excitement."

"Some children put their hands up at every opportunity," Adams says, "while others won't, even if they know the answers."

But the Bridlington Brain Trust has a solution. They want students to respond by giving a "thumbs-up" instead.

(I hope they warn the kiddies not to try that in Australia, Argentina and especially in Iran, where a thumbs-up means a thumbs-up-yours.)

They also better not try it any schoolrooms in Ionia, Michigan. Schools there have a "zero tolerance policy." Translated, that means they are politically correct to the point of insanity. A student by the name of Mason Jammer made the thumbs-up sign to a classmate in an Ionia public school recently. His teacher decided he was "imitating a revolver" and had him suspended and sent home. Mason Jammer is six years old.

Sad, sad, sad. I'm with author Ellen Gilchrist who said: "All you have to do to educate a child is to leave them alone and teach them to read. The rest is brainwashing."

Watch Your Mouth!

Y ou like it hot and sticky? Have I got a party place for you. Rent-free, for starters, plus a constant temperature of thirty-five degrees Celsius, 100 percent humidity—and all the food you can eat.

Not a bad gig—for a bacterium.

We're talking about your mouth and what's living in there. By the end of this missive you may never French kiss again. Even if you brush three times a day and cut your Johnny Walker with Listerine, you are a virtual slum landlord when it comes to your pie hole. You've got bacteria, fungi, protozoa and sundry viruses of no fixed address hanging out between your teeth, just under your gums, on your tongue—even on the roof of your mouth. The bad news is: you'll never get rid of them. The good news is: you really don't want to. Most of these wriggly critters are Good Guys. They'd be wearing Mountie stetsons if we made hat sizes that small. They toil away 24/7, hunting down and knocking off bad bacteria—when they're not nibbling on the bits of cheeseburger and corn dog stuck between our teeth.

Then there's the Bad Guys. Not a lot of them, really, but enough to ruin a neighbourhood. We call them the Strep Gang (full name *Streptococcus mutans*). The Strep Gang members used to be Good Guys but we got them hooked on drugs and now they've gone rogue. The drug that did them in? Refined sugar.

See, for most of our history we didn't have refined sugar—and had better teeth for it. Back in the old days, chemicals in our saliva routinely neutralized acids from raw sugar. But *Streptococcus mutans* goes ape for the new fancy-pants refined sugar—which it converts into acid that attacks tooth enamel and eventually produces those canyons, arroyos, wadis, coulees and black holes we call cavities.

The solution? Way less sugar of course—and good luck with that. The North American diet is saturated in refined sugars to the point of obscenity (check out the adulterated breakfast cereals aimed exclusively at kids—Sugar Frosted Flakes . . . Count Chocula . . . who needs that crap?).

Then of course there's candy. We have that annual sugar orgy called Halloween, in which kids vie with one another to see how many garbage bags of sweets they can amass—chocolate bars, toffee, peanut brittle, peppermints, butterscotch, licorice, jelly beans, jawbreakers, Life Savers, candy kisses, candy canes, bubble gum . . .

Oh, hold it on the gum. Turns out that gum is good for kids. In fact, it turns out gum is exactly what our candy-overdosing kids need.

I'm not making that up. A dental study in Finland way back in the 1980s revealed that kids who chewed gum had 60 percent fewer cavities than kids who didn't. A more recent study in Belize found even better numbers—70 percent fewer cavities among gum-chewing ten year olds. Not just any gum of course. It has to be sweetened with xylitol, a naturally occurring sweetener present in many fruits and vegetables.

Dental experts are now recommending that children *be encouraged* to chew gum in school, three times a day, starting in kindergarten.

Ironic. As a kid I got my knuckles whacked for chewing gum in school. If I were a student now, I'd be nailed for NOT chewing gum in school.

Ah well. As that eminent philosopher Alfred E. Neuman said: "We live in a world where lemonade is made from artificial flavours and furniture polish is made from real lemons."

Now there's something to chew on.

To *P* or Not to *P*

I'm having a wee problem with the sixteenth letter of the alphabet. You know—the one between *O* and *Q*.

Right . . . it's *P*, or more specifically in my case, Pee.

Peeing is something I've done several times every day of my life but I'm still getting mixed messages about it.

When I was a kid I risked anything from a dressing down to a cuff upside the head if I didn't wash my hands immediately following the deed. This taught me that urine is a dangerous substance and a threat to my health and well-being.

Then I found out that Mahatma Gandhi drank the stuff.

Really. He downed a glass of his own urine every morning. Couldn't have been too toxic—he died at seventy-nine.

And not just Gandhi. Ancient Romans brushed their teeth with their own urine to brighten their smiles. French in the Renaissance wore scarves soaked in urine to ward off strep throat. The Chinese have practised urine therapy for a variety of maladies for centuries. It's advocated in the Hindu scriptures where it's known as *amaroli*. Even the King James Bible promotes urine therapy ("Drink waters from thy own cistern." Proverbs 5:15).

Not just the ancients either. Moises Alou, the one-time Montreal Expos baseball star, claimed he pees on his hands to prevent calluses. Madonna confided to David Letterman (and his audience of millions) that she pees on her feet to alleviate athlete's foot.

So which is it—a foul body-waste product or the golden elixir of life? Some medical specialists still consider it a potentially dangerous commodity, but don't try to tell that to Old MacDonald down on the farm.

Turns out I've been neglecting my garden by not peeing on it. I know a rose grower in my neighbourhood (no names to protect the piddler) who anoints his rose bushes on a regular basis. He says his personal daily blessing results in luxurious prize-winning blooms year after year. Agronomists in Finland claim that a combination of urine and wood ash resulted in a whopping 400 percent increase in tomatoes, and a report in the *Washington Post* credits the application of human urine for a fantastic increase in cabbage yields.

Makes sense when you think about it. Urine is rich in potassium, nitrogen and phosphate—just like those bags of fertilizer you pay an arm and a leg for at the gardening store.

Mind you, urine is also highly acidic so you have to apply it judiciously. Fortunately for males the dispenser is, um, flexible. Professionals advise applicators to "keep moving," so to speak.

Reminds me of the story I heard in an English pub years ago. Seems Lord Grantham, a local member of the aristocracy, had been shot by an irate husband.

"What did he do?" I asked the bartender.

"He was walking in the garden with Lady Cynthia, the other man's wife," he said.

I pointed out that that a mere walk in a garden with another man's wife seemed harmless enough.

The bartender polished a glass. "Yes," he said, "but you see, it was snowing. During the walk Lord Grantham paused to relieve himself. They found his name 'written' in the snow."

I allowed as how that was eccentric, frivolous, and possibly tasteless—but hardly a shooting offence.

The bartender shook his head, leaned in and whispered, "You don't understand. The signature was in Lady Cynthia's handwriting."

Road Rage: A Handy Guide

It was a sweltering midsummer day and I was stopped at a traffic light. The AC was on the fritz so I had all the car windows open.

Otherwise, I probably wouldn't have heard the cursing.

It came from the car behind me. I could see the driver's face in my mirror. It was deep magenta, his eyes were bulging, the veins in his neck standing out like sail shrouds. He was leaning toward his front passenger window, directing a Niagara of expletives at the people in the car alongside him. In that car sat a frail and elderly couple, frozen in fear, staring straight ahead.

I don't know the nature of the old folks' driving infraction, real or imagined, but the berserker's reaction was absurdly over the top. What made it extra ugly was the little boy sitting beside the driver—his son, presumably—also staring straight ahead.

Nice lesson in civility, Dad.

Road rage. What a weird phenomenon. Where did it come from? Was there such a thing as horse-and-buggy rage? Roman chariot rage?

Probably. Where there's testosterone, there's a way. The term, however, is only a few decades old, originating back in the 1980s as a description for a rash of car-to-car shootings that occurred on the freeways around Los Angeles. Road rage doesn't always involve firearms. It can manifest as verbal abuse, rude and menacing gestures or simply aggressive driving.

Had a case of it myself, once, many years ago. A younger, stupider version of yours truly was tooling down Highway 401 north of Toronto. I blew by a middle-aged dawdler in a station wagon, not thinking much about it. A few seconds later I looked over and there he was beside me, hunched over his steering wheel, driving fender to fender, determined to pass.

Was I sensible? Did I hit the brakes and let him have his way, tut-tutting him with a mild finger wave?

I mentioned "younger and stupider," right? I floored it; he floored it; I floored it some more. We both hurtled down the highway at probably twice the speed limit, both of us white-knuckling the wheel, determined that We'd Show That Jerk.

Nothing tragic happened. There were no rollovers, no caroming off the guardrails or wailing cop sirens. My exit eventually came up and I took it. As my car and my heart slowed down in tandem I remember thinking: what the hell was that about?

I still wonder.

Why did the doofus in the station wagon feel he suddenly needed to risk his life to pass me? Why did I feel I had to risk my life to prevent him? That's the scary thing about road rage: it makes no sense at all. Some drivers describe "a red mist" swirling before their eyes and an overpowering urge to "get even" at any cost.

The typical road rager? Male. Single. Spotty education. Mid-level income.

And of course, young. Usually under thirty-five.

Usually, but not always. Clyde White of Corbin, Kentucky, recently ran afoul of the law. The cops finally collared him, but not until the conclusion of a chase that reached speeds of over a hundred miles per hour. And not before White had rammed two other cars with his own. One of the rammed cars was driven by his brother, aged eighty-two; the other by his sister, aged eighty-three.

Clyde himself is seventy-eight. Proving that when it comes to road rage, it doesn't matter if you're young or old.

Just as long as you're stupid.

Too Much to Bear

Nowhere in a zoo can a stranger encounter the look of an animal. At most the animal's gaze flickers and passes on. They look sideways. They look blindly beyond.

—JOHN BERGER

I acquired an early distaste for zoos when I was just a kid, maybe ten or twelve. My dad stopped for gas at a Hicksville service station/ greasy spoon just north of Toronto on Highway 27. Near the pump I spied a crudely lettered wooden sign that said "BEAR," with an arrow pointing toward the back of the garage. I followed the arrow and came upon what looked like an old wino in a scruffy wool coat.

Turned out to be Tiny, a sad-eyed brown bear stuck in a cage that was hardly big enough for him to turn around in.

That's what Tiny the Bear did—turn around. Around and around and around. He didn't look at me, he ignored the wieners and dough-nuts visitors had tossed in the cage. He just turned around and around.

Oh, I know that modern zoos have come a long way since Tiny's time. Nowadays the enclosures are bigger and more "natural"; the animals—in this country at least—are well-fed and cared for by professionals.

But they're still inmates; they're still in prison.

It's a conundrum. We continue to clear-cut, subdivide and pave their natural habitat, so what's the alternative—let them starve? No, better to "relocate" them to the safer environment of a zoo—sorry: a "monitored wildlife refuge."

You know—like we did with the Indians when we stole *their* land.

I hadn't thought about Tiny in years. What brought him back to my mind was a story about another bear, named Clover, presently residing at a wildlife centre near Smithers, BC. Clover's only about a year and a half but he comes from a broken home and he's already got a rap sheet. His mother was shot by hunters and Clover subsequently broke into a shack at an archaeology camp looking for food. Campers had been tempting him with food so they could take his picture, but never mind. Clover was now into breaking and entering and that is usually the kiss of death for any wild bear. Once they associate humans with food, they become too unpredictable. Indeed, when conservation officers trapped Clover they fully intended to shoot him on the spot. Only one thing saved him.

Clover is pure white.

He's a kermode or spirit bear—a black bear with a rare genetic trait that renders his coat a creamy white. There are fewer than a thousand—perhaps as few as four hundred—spirit bears in the world and they all live in British Columbia's central and north coast wilderness. The fact that there are any spirit bears at all is probably due to the protection of First Nations people who have always held them in high esteem. They neither hunted them nor mentioned their existence to Russian or European fur traders and trappers.

Clover's life will be spared too, but his roving days are done. Bears can't be "un-trained" from looking to humans for food.

So Clover will spend the rest of his life at the BC Wildlife Park in Kamloops. Folks there are excited. They've set out to raise half a million dollars to construct a new bear facility just for Clover.

"I anticipate enormous public interest," says general manager Glenn Grant. "It's hard to quantify in dollars or visits, but we know there will be tour companies that will want to come to Kamloops to see this bear."

Lucky Clover.

C'mon Canada—Do the Locomotion

*If you think North Americans are a vigorous people . . .
just watch the natives in the business centre of any
United States town. They'd rather park illegally, pay a
fine or go to jail than leave their cars two blocks away
and walk to their destination.*

—ARMANDO PIRES

Do you ever get depressed? Angry? Tired? Confused? Then throw your hat in the air and your meds out the window because scientists at Essex University in the UK have identified a simple physiological cure that they claim dramatically reduces anger, confusion, fatigue and depression in humans.

That's the good news. The better news is, it's universally accessible, easy to master, non-addictive, safe when taken as directed and cheap as borscht.

They call it walking.

Really. A team of Essex U. researchers tracked a study group of 1,252 walkers (various ages, men and women, dispositions ranging from happy to gloomy). The assignment was a simple one: get off your duff and go for a walk. Every day. In natural surroundings—in a park, along a riverbank, through a forest if it was handy.

The results were gobsmacking. Seventy-nine percent of the participants reported feeling more "centred," 86 percent said they were less tense and 92 percent claimed they felt "happier"—even after a short walk.

That was the biggest surprise. These walkers didn't traverse the Scottish Highlands or rappel down a cliff face in Wales. They went for short, gentle strolls well away from the bright lights. Researchers found that people's mood, self-esteem and overall mental health showed an improvement after just five minutes of simply walking in the woods. The most profoundly affected? Young people and folks with mental health issues—but absolutely everybody got a buzz.

The Japanese have recognized this phenomenon for some time. Living in one of the most paved-over, built-up and altogether urbanized nations in the world has perhaps made them appreciate their precious green spaces more than Canadians.

That's why so many Japanese have taken up the practice of *shin-rin-ryoho*. Literally, it means forest therapy.

In practice, it means going for a walk in the bush. According to a report in *The Globe and Mail*, there are forty official forest therapy sites in Japan. They plan to increase that to over a hundred in the next decade. Citizens are encouraged to come with their families or alone and immerse themselves for a few minutes—or hours—by going for a walk in surroundings conspicuously lacking sidewalks, roadways, vehicular traffic, concrete, neon or seething throngs of harassed humanity feverishly waiting for the lights to change.

The researchers at Essex U. basically discovered what is old news to the Japanese.

North America, please copy.

We don't walk much on this continent. Even the urban Japanese average 7,168 steps a day. Adults in Western Australia are the world champs. They take an average of 9,695 steps a day. Americans limp in at a little better than half that—5,117 steps per Yank per day.

Canucks aren't exactly marathon class either. A study published in *Health Reports* shows that 41 percent of us—nearly eleven million sluggos—admit to walking less than a half-hour per week to get to school or work or do errands. That goes a long way toward explaining why the same study shows that one in three Canucks over the age of twenty is clinically overweight.

One-third of us. Check out the folks standing (more likely sitting) on either side of you. If they're both skinny—then it's you.

The beauty of the walking cure is it's cheap and simple. You don't have to get a doctor's certificate, join a health club or buy expensive gear. Just pull on a pair of sneakers and start putting one foot in front of the other.

It's never too late, but a word of warning: results can be unexpected.

Take my Uncle Vernon. Big smoker. Heavy drinker. Seriously overweight. On his sixty-first birthday he made a resolution to do something about it. He started out walking just one mile a day.

That was just three weeks ago. Now we don't know where the hell he is.

Where There's Smoke, There's Ire

Have you spotted any lately? They frequently travel in packs of three or four, but just as often they're solo. You see them clustered around the entrances of bars, restaurants, hospitals, office buildings and the like. They're easy to identify by their furtive gestures, hunched shoulders and darting glances over their shoulders.

CBC Radio icon Peter Gzowski once interviewed some visiting Russians who had encountered packs of these creatures bunched around the doorways of hospitals in the Far North. "It is a great pity, the number of prostitutes in your North," one Russian lamented solemnly.

Gzowski laughed. "Those aren't prostitutes—they're smokers."

Small wonder that Canada's nicotine addicts have been reduced to the behaviour of urban coyotes—there are fewer and fewer places they can indulge. Smoking is forbidden at the zoo in Peterborough, Ontario; at beaches in Vancouver, White Rock, Arnprior and Orillia; next to building entrances in all of Alberta, the Yukon, Nova Scotia and British Columbia.

As for smoking in restaurants, I'm not sure if there's any place in the country where you can still light up and order a meal at the same time.

I'm not complaining, you understand. As a reformed nicomaniac, I'm just as self-righteous and intolerant of public smoking as the next person. I'm just saying that anybody who still smokes has got it particularly tough in this era of cancer-conscious, clean-air-zealous, extreme tobacco hostility.

Not to mention having to fork over ten dollars for a small pack of gaspers.

It's more like fifteen bucks a pack if you buy your smokes in New York City. In an effort to reduce still further the number of New York smokers, Gotham mayor Michael Bloomberg has jacked up tobacco taxes to levels that would make a crack dealer blush.

But New Yorkers are an inventive lot. There's a place on Staten Island where you can buy your fix for only $2.95 a pack.

But this is New York, so there's a catch, natch.

You have to roll the cigarettes yourself.

The helpful folks at Island Smokes will assist you. There's a cigarette-stuffing machine on site and mounds of pipe tobacco (it's taxed at a lower rate than cigarette tobacco). You sit on a wooden stool alongside up to a dozen other hard-core smokers, insert an empty cigarette paper into a hole, press a button and out the other end comes a rolled smoke. Takes about four seconds per unit.

It's a tiny, legalistic loophole that the proprietors of Island Smokes are exploiting and it probably won't last forever. City lawyers have already slammed the owners with a cease-and-desist order; the tax gendarmes have dropped by and informed them that they are in violation of at least three city bylaws.

Another radio icon, Garrison Keillor, once wrote a short story about the Last of the Smokers, in which America's final desperate, defiant clutch of smokers were hunted down, captured and rehabilitated by the minions of decency. It was a Swiftian satirical piece of writing, deliberately exaggerating the plight of smokers to the point of absurdity.

Or maybe not.

Yet another writer (and smoker) thought and wrote about the filthy vice. Kurt Vonnegut defined the habit of smoking cigarettes as "a socially acceptable form of suicide."

Vonnegut had a black sense of humour. He died, still smoking unfiltered Pall Malls, at the age of eighty-four.

But with a wicked smoker's cough, I'll bet.

Shakespeare the Spin Doctor

*The evil that men do lives after them; the good is oft
interred with their bones.*

—WILLIAM SHAKESPEARE

Ah yes. The enduring fame of infamy. Names of monsters like
Karla Homolka and Clifford Olson are etched on our minds for
life, but . . . that woman who pulled three kids from a burning house?
What was her name again?

Which brings us to Richard.

A time bomb of a handle to lumber a kid with, and not just because
of its unfortunate diminutive, "Dick."

Richard conjures up the spectre of *Richard III*, one of Shakespeare's
earlier plays. In the Bard's estimation, Richard III was emphatically
Not a Nice Guy.

In Shakespeare's telling, King Richard has Henry VI murdered
along with his son. Richard also offs his wife Anne Neville, his own
brother George, sundry other royals and, most infamously, the two
little princes—twelve-year-old Edward and nine-year-old Richard.
What a beast, *n'est-ce pas?*

But what if it never happened? What if Richard III, instead of
being England's most vilified monarch, was merely a victim of Tudor
spin doctors?

Could be. The dynasty that replaced Richard III made a habit of
blaming everything they could on the previous administration (sound
familiar?) and when it came to political slander, a certain young

playwright from Stratford-upon-Avon, who came along a century or so later, turned out to be the Karl Rove of his time. Richard suffered from a slight curvature of the spine; Shakespeare turned him into a brooding hunchback. Shakespeare has King Richard killing the Duke of Somerset at the Battle of St. Albans. No mean feat. Richard would have been two years old at the time.

Indeed, there is no evidence that Richard was guilty of any of the killings Shakespeare attributes to him. As for the murder of the princes in the tower, experts agree that no modern court would convict Richard of the crime. Any number of royal court intriguers could have benefited from the disappearance of the princes—most especially Richard's successor, Henry VII. If Richard had a better PR department he might be regarded today not as a blot on the royal escutcheon but as a champion of the people— he abolished press censorship, established the right to bail for people awaiting trial, cleaned up England's finances and even performed heroically in battle, despite his physical frailty. A historian of the time records that "to his last breath he held himself nobly in a defending manner."

Unfortunately, Richard not only lost his life at Bosworth, he lost the battle too. And it's the victors who get to write the history books.

Reminds me of a certain US president who tried to remake America. He created a vast network of federal grants to state and local governments that cost billions. He set up a national agency to regulate pollution; another to guard workers' health and safety. He even tried to bring in a guaranteed minimum wage and a national health plan for low-income families. Like Richard III, his time in office was cut short.

Odd thing: his name was Richard too—Richard Milhous Nixon.

Makes you think.

Ice Fishing in the Olympics?

We can all agree that the Olympics have become utterly silly, right? Synchronized swimming has always been goofy; beach volleyball is a voyeur's wet dream, aimed, it would seem, at attracting an audience of creepy guys in stained raincoats who normally hang out in peep show arcades. And equestrian dressage? Please. Are there eleven people *in the world* who have ever sat through an entire episode of equestrian dressage televised coverage?

There was a time when the Olympics were serious. I have stood on the track at Olympia in Greece where athletes of antiquity vied to see who was the fastest runner, the wiliest wrestler, the most agile gymnast. Those Olympic Games were simple and straightforward; but that was two thousand years ago. The modern Olympic Games are a travelling circus of civic hoopla, media sensationalism and under-the-table corruption and graft. The athletes today are all but an afterthought amid the wining and dining and wheeling and dealing that constitutes the modern Olympic experience.

And now the seedy backroom boys who run the Olympics are on the verge of lowering the Olympics bar to limbo depths: they are considering making ice fishing an Olympic sport.

Really. Last winter (you may have missed it) the World Ice Fishing Championship was held in Wisconsin, and when it was over, the US Anti-Doping Agency rounded up the contestants.

To test their urine for the presence of steroids and/or growth hormones.

Trust me: there are no drugs in ice fishing. Unless beer counts.

I spent my formative winters not far from the ice-fishing hotbed (okay, not hot) of Lake Simcoe in Southern Ontario. I also spent more than a dozen winters in and around Thunder Bay. I am somewhat of an expert on ice fishing.

But that's not saying much. Can you bait a hook? Can you hold a line? Can you sit for hours cultivating hemorrhoids over a hole on a frozen lake waiting for a tug to jerk you out of your frozen torpor? Hey! You're an ice-fishing expert too.

Ice fishing is what you do when you can't stand being cooped up in your log cabin anymore. It ain't, as the saying goes, rocket surgery. It also isn't an Olympic sport. A Holstein could be a successful ice fisher. Except Holsteins have more sense.

Not that there isn't a certain amount of cunning involved. I recall the time I was ice fishing on Lake Nipigon years ago and not having any luck at all. Along comes an old guy with an axe, a bucket and a grubby old haversack. He chops a hole in the ice about twenty metres away, baits a hook, drops in a line—and within minutes he's hauling in fish after fish.

I haven't had a nibble.

After half an hour I can't stand it anymore. I walk over and ask him what his secret is. He glares up at me and mumbles: "Roo affa heep ah wums wahm!"

I say, "Sorry? Come again?"

"Roo affa heep ah wums wahm!"

I tell him I still can't understand what he's saying.

He spits a slimy brown ball into his mitten and says:

"You have to keep your worms warm!"

PART SEVEN

Man vs. Machine: Who's Winning?

Ruins: The New Pornography

A couple of hundred years ago a poet by the name of Percy Bysshe Shelley scribbled down fourteen lines that would eventually become his most famous poem. It told of a traveller in desert lands coming across the ruins of what was once a colossal statue honouring a long-forgotten ruler. The inscription on what was left of the pedestal read:

> My name is Ozymandias, king of kings:
> Look on my works, ye Mighty, and despair

Except there were no mighty works to look at. The Ozymandian empire, however vast and magnificent it might once have been, had crumbled to a few chunks of marble half-buried in desert sand. No one even remembered who Ozymandias was.

Some ruins fare better. We do our best to understand and preserve what's left of the pyramids of Egypt, the monoliths of Stonehenge, the Athenian Acropolis and the Roman Colosseum. Here in North America we're a little short on architectural antiquities, but we have some pretty impressive ruins all the same. As a matter of fact we have a stunning collection right in the centre of the continent, just a hop, skip and a tunnel ride from Windsor, Ontario.

It's called Detroit.

It used to be known as Motor City but that was in better days when gas was cheap and everybody lusted for a new car every year. Today, it's more like Mouldering City. More than half the population—about one million citizens—have left the city since its heyday back in the 1960s. Seventy thousand buildings have been abandoned and trashed—some of them heartbreakingly magnificent even in their downfall. Michigan Central Station is—was—eighteen storeys of fabulous beaux-arts design with vaulting arches and marble pillars. Today, it is home to junkies, rats and cockroaches. The Vanity Ballroom, which once rocked to the rhythms of the Duke Ellington and Tommy Dorsey orchestras, has been disembowelled by vandals. It now lies gutted of its brass, velvet and mahogany, carpeted in broken glass, its art deco chandelier incongruously intact.

The presence of a visibly decaying metropolis in our midst has given rise to a new and somewhat perverted form of tourism. It's called Ruin Porn. YouTube is awash with photo displays of some of Detroit's more spectacular failures. Tourist buses full of out-of-town rubberneckers crawl through the decimated neighbourhoods that are now disappearing into jungles of chickweed and scrub brush, the passengers tut-tutting while click-clicking their smart phones. An entrepreneur has arranged to cater gourmet meals served by highbrow chefs in abandoned buildings such as the formerly opulent 3.5-million-square-foot Packard plant that used to churn out automobiles.

Is there an upside to the fall of Detroit? Well, some claim the city is on the brink of reinventing itself. Citizens who haven't fled to more salubrious climes are planting crops and raising chickens in what used to be parking lots and schoolyards. One born-again Detroit pioneer says, "Look on the bright side. We don't have hurricanes like the East Coast. We don't have droughts like the West . . . Plus, I bought a Mies van der Rohe townhouse downtown for just $100,000."

On the other hand, it is still Detroit, a.k.a. Murder City. A recent crime report told of an early-morning multiple shooting following which the perpetrator turned himself in at a Detroit fire station. The firemen called the police several times to come and arrest the guy. The police, for reasons best known to themselves, declined to respond.

So the firefighters took up a collection, put the man in a taxi and sent him to the police station.

I wonder if Percy Shelley could find a poem in that.

Cementing Relationships

A few years back, William Kinsella, one of Canada's finer short story writers, was attending a reading by Canada's—and probably the world's—finest short story writer, Alice Munro. Kinsella noticed a curious thing. As Munro read, the audience laughed repeatedly and uproariously. Reading audiences are normally about as jovial as Stephen Harper with mumps. After the reading, Kinsella mentioned it to Munro and said that he'd never thought of her work as funny. Munro smiled and said, "Bill, *everything* is funny."

Well, exactly. Take cement. Superficially, few things could be less funny than cement. It is bland, undifferentiated, mostly grey, the epitome of unsexy—again, like Stephen Harper.

But unsexy doesn't mean unimportant. Bland old boring cement is the elemental binder of human architecture. Without cement we wouldn't have the Taj Mahal, Chartres Cathedral or the George Massey Tunnel. Builders figured that out centuries ago. The ancient Romans even gave us our word for it. They call the mixture of crushed rock and burnt limestone they used *opus caementicium*.

So cement is a certifiable big deal—but funny?

Actually, yes.

Cement plays a critical role in one of my favourite barroom stories. A ready-mix truck driver stops by his home during a work run to discover a shiny Cadillac convertible parked in his driveway. He tiptoes to the bedroom window, peeks in, discovers his wife is entertaining a strange man within. Tiptoes back to his cement truck, backs it up to the Cadillac, places the chute in back seat of Cadillac and dumps his load.

Such a satisfying story—almost too good to be true. In fact, it IS too good to be true. It's an urban legend that's been making the rounds for the past forty years at least. Sometimes the cement-filled car is a Cadillac, other times it's a Mercedes or a Triumph TR3. Some people insist it actually happened to Don Tyson, president of Tyson Foods, Inc. That story goes that Tyson's wife spied her husband's expensive new Cadillac parked in the driveway of another woman's house, so she ordered up a load of concrete and had it delivered—through the passenger's side window.

Except it never happened. In 1992 the Public Relations department of Tyson Foods, Inc., officially declared the story to be a fake. They also said they'd been hearing it for at least twenty years.

Great story. Too bad it never happened. But here's one that did: on a highway outside San Francisco, an impatient guy in a Porsche 911 found himself at the end of a long line of cars that weren't moving. He honked, he shook his fist, he said several bad words—then he put his car in first gear and drove around the line of cars.

Right into a lane of freshly poured cement. The Porsche sank about a foot before it came to a rather final stop.

True story—and it reminds me of another barroom story. Guy is tooling along a country road in his Porsche, well over the speed limit, comes over a rise and hits a cow broadside. When the cops show up the guy is standing, bleeding, by his totalled sports car wailing, "My Porsche! My beautiful Porsche!"

The cop says, "You yuppies make me puke. You're flying down the road, way over the speed limit; you kill an innocent cow—and look, you tore your right arm off! And all you can think about is your Porsche???"

Guy looks at his empty right sleeve and wails, "My Rolex! My beautiful Rolex!"

Older but Dumber

Here's a sobering thought: we are all, collectively, dumber than we were three millennia ago.

Not my idea—it belongs to Gerald Crabtree, a research geneticist at Stanford University. Dr. Crabtree posits that if an average citizen from the city of Athens, circa 1000 BC, were to be dropped, *Star Trek* teleportation-style, into modern-day life "he or she would be among the brightest and most intellectually alive of our colleagues and companions."

What? Ancient Greeks were smarter than twenty-first-century citizens? Impossible! Consider the relative levels of sophistication. We modern *Homo sapiens* have eighteen-wheel semis, iPads and waterproof Tilley safari jackets. The ancient Greeks rode donkeys, wrote on wax tablets and wore bed sheets.

On the other hand, those old Greeks had Plato, Socrates and Aristotle. We have Donald Trump, Rob Ford and Sarah Palin.

Dr. Crabtree says we're dumber today because we no longer need to be smart the way we used to. Back in the Bad Old Days, if you didn't figure out a way to keep the sabre-toothed tiger out of your cave or ensure that your family was warm and well-fed the results were, um, profound. Back then, to be dumb was to be dead. Mother Nature, unsentimental matriarch that she is, had no qualms about pruning deadwood from the family tree.

"A hunter-gatherer who did not correctly conceive a solution to providing food or shelter probably died," says Crabtree, "whereas a modern Wall Street executive that made a similar conceptual mistake would receive a substantial bonus and be a more attractive mate."

Case in point: the aforementioned Mr. Trump, a blow-dried baboon who's been bankrupt more times than Lindsay Lohan's been arrested, has his own TV show and a personal line of cologne.

Some people want to *smell* like Donald Trump?? Explain that, Darwin.

But, ancient Athenian or contemporary Canuck, there's no question that we are, for better or worse, the dominant species on Planet Earth. And how did we pull that off? We can't soar like eagles, run like cheetahs, swim like orcas or out-wrestle a grizzly. Physically we are comparatively pallid, puny and more than a little pathetic. So what do we have that our fellow earth tenants lack? What do we do that they don't do?

Simple. We cook.

Heating food—be it meat or vegetable—breaks down the cellular structure, which speeds up chewing and digestion. That means the human body absorbs more nutrition with each bite. Watch a cow or a robin or a gopher for a while. They spend most of their time chewing or pecking or grazing whatever they can find to chew, peck or graze. Other creatures are forced to eat or look for food virtually all their waking hours, but not us. About two million years ago some anonymous caveman accidentally dropped a bleeding chunk of mammoth haunch into the fire and discovered the secret of cooking. That changed everything. Researchers reckon that had our *Homo erectus* ancestors eaten only a raw food diet they would have had to spend more than nine hours every day just eating and digesting food to feed their over-large brains.

So, nine hours for digestion, say, eight hours for sleep, and enough other hours every day to build fires, avoid predators, find shelter, forage for food . . .

That doesn't leave much time to invent the wheel.

Fortunately, we stumbled upon the concept of cooking. That bought us time—time to invent language and art and science and . . . and . . .

Have you met the Segway? It was invented in our lifetime—only unveiled in 2001, as a matter of fact. The experts promised it would revolutionize transportation around the world.

It's a two-wheeled scooter built along the lines of a push lawn mower. You stand on it, tilt the handle in the direction you want to travel and off you go, at a stately ten miles per hour. The Segway is compact, environmentally friendly, very safe (George W. Bush fell off his, but . . .) and cheap.

Well, pretty cheap. I saw one on eBay for six grand.

Yep, the Segway is a transportation dream come true—except hardly anyone likes them. Because when you stand on a Segway you look like a dork.

I know I'm going to get emails from the eleven Segway owners in Canada saying that I've maligned the vehicle and it's really a sexy ride.

I respect your position. All I'm saying is Socrates would have thought you looked ridiculous.

Rule Britannica! Not

If there was any skepticism about the digital information tsunami we're currently dog-paddling through, surely it was swept away by the terse announcement that recently appeared in newspapers, magazines—and inevitably on iPads and laptop screens around the world. I'm referring to the one telling us that after 244 years of publishing, *Encyclopedia Britannica* would no longer be putting out a print edition.

No more *Encyclopedia Britannica*? No more of those glossy-paged, gold-embossed, hernia-inducing, faux-leather volumes that have anchored libraries, private and public, since . . . since Oliver Goldsmith scribbled, William Hogarth doodled and Catherine the Great diddled?

Well, pardon the hysteria. This is a death notice that was not exactly unexpected. Truth is, *Britannica*'s been on the endangered list since at least 1990 when the company declared bankruptcy, only to be temporarily rescued by a Swiss businessman. Even before that, *Encyclopedia Britannica* was coasting on the fumes of an inflated reputation. The information its volumes contained was often outdated before they were printed. The latest (and last) print edition, published in 2010, was *twenty-five years* in the making.

But it wasn't just the information lag that doomed the print version of the *Encyclopedia Britannica*. Consider: if you were one of the eight thousand customers who purchased the latest edition, you would have thirty-two volumes that would take up a wall of your house, weigh 130 pounds and set you back nearly $1,400.

Or, for seventy bucks a year, you could subscribe to the web edition and enjoy instant access in your bedroom, a bus terminal or an Internet café.

But that's today. Back in the days when we weren't in a perpetual rush and portability wasn't a concern, *Encyclopedia Britannica* ruled.

Ruled the middle class, anyway. And it never really was about information; it was about social status. Families that boasted a set of EBs in their parlour ascended automatically to the mandarin class. And it didn't matter whether anyone actually *opened* a volume. The books just had to be there, where visitors could see them. When people purchased *Britannicas* they weren't just buying information; they were buying a dream.

I know. I used to sell that dream.

I was once a door-to-door encyclopedia salesman. On my first evening, clad in an ill-fitting sports jacket and tie, I tagged along behind a seasoned salesman who would show me the ropes. By "seasoned" I mean sleazy. This guy was a weasel in a suit. We knocked on every door in a large downtown high-rise. I lugged a satchel full of sales gimmickry. Weasel did the talking.

Virtually all of the doors we knocked on were either unanswered or curtly slammed in our faces. But finally, some poor, kind soul whose mother taught her not to be rude to strangers invited us in.

Big mistake.

The weasel had a polished line of patter that bordered on hypnotic. He dazzled the little old dear like a cobra bewitching a sparrow. Before an hour was gone she had signed up not only for an overpriced set of *Britannicas* but also for a bookcase, a reading lamp and a subscription for an annual update volume.

We were operating inside the law, but just barely. And morally what we were doing sucked large granite boulders. I was just a kid then, and not nearly brave enough to stand up and shout, "Close your chequebook, lady—it's a scam!" But I often wish I had. My encyclopedia sales career began and ended that same night. The experience soured me on what I had considered to be a noble institution. After all, how noble could *Encyclopedia Britannica* be if it employed two-bit hustlers like us?

I don't believe I've cracked the spine on a volume of *Encyclopedia Britannica* since.

But then, neither have lots of people who bought the whole set.

Whatever Happened to Email?

It's safe to assume that no one alive has ever seen a quagga. The last specimen died in an Amsterdam zoo in 1883. Quaggas, a kind of half-zebra, half-horse combo, used to roam southern Africa in huge, dense herds but they're extinct now, just like T. Rex, the dodo and email.

Beg pardon? Email? Extinct? Well, almost, according to Atos, Europe's largest information technology firm. The company claims that 90 percent of email messages sent among its employees are a waste of time and money. Accordingly, Atos employees—all seventy-four thousand of them—have been ordered to ditch the email and go back to the telephone. Email was supposed to boost office productivity; in fact, it's behaved like cholesterol, clogging the arteries of the business machine. Think of all the crap emails you get. Think of the millions of people who, like you, take time out to at least glance at their crap emails. Studies show useless emails can cost a company of one thousand employees as much as ten million dollars a year.

Ah, well. We're getting used to extinctions these days. Tyrannosaurus Rex terrorized the river valleys of Western Canada for a couple of million years during the Upper Cretaceous period before flaming out, whereas, say, the Polaroid Land Camera barely lasted sixty years (1948–2007) before being flung into the Landfill of History.

And remember the pager? Back in the 1980s it was hard to find a doctor or a salesman who didn't have one clipped on his or her belt. One or two rappers even went briefly pager-crazy in their performances. Then along came the mobile phone to gobble it up. RIP, noble pager.

And who doesn't have a Sony Walkman gathering dust at the back of a drawer? When they first appeared in the early '80s Walkmans drove a stake through the heart (or the centre hole) of phonograph LPs. Then, just a few years ago, along came a mutation called the iPod, and the Sony Walkman went straight to the Museum of Quaint Artifacts.

It had lots of company. The PalmPilot, born in 1997, was a wonder of its time. Imagine having all your contacts, an accurate calendar and personal notes in one handy gizmo! With a touch screen and a personal stylus to boot! What could possibly improve on that?

A company named Apple for one. Hello iPhone; adios PalmPilot.

Then there's the Atari 2600. Customers snapped up more than thirty million of those to play video games like Pong, Pitfall and Combat. For all its fame Atari lived for only seven years: 1977–84.

All these techno dinosaurs share two characteristics. Number one: they were each once on the very knife-edge of surging technology, worth hundreds of millions of dollars. Number two: their collapse was utter and lightning-swift in evolutionary terms. Thirty years for the Sony Walkman. A decade for the PalmPilot. Seven years for Atari.

And now we're watching the titanic struggles (which look increasingly like death throes) of Canada's own BlackBerry. Just a couple of years ago it was the world leader in smart phones, commanding over 50 percent of the American market alone. That share is now down to 10 percent and circling the drain.

But evolution's like a baseball game: it's not over until the last at-bat. Back in the mid-1990s, a company named Apple was on the ropes too. They appointed a guy named Steve Jobs as CEO.

They did all right.

As for email, the prognosis isn't bright. "The younger generation has all but given up on it," says a feature story in the *London Daily Mail*—in favour of social networks like Facebook and Twitter. Why? Instant messaging feels more "immediate." Messages don't languish unread in somebody's inbox. In fact with Twitter, it can feel almost like you're having an actual, one-on-one conversation with somebody.

A face-to-face conversation. You can remember what that was like, can't you?

Riding on Spaceship Earth

Ever try to make a map? It's a tough assignment that ought to give us that much more respect for pioneers like Marco Polo, Magellan and our own Samuel de Champlain—all dedicated map-makers who took pains to leave a record of where they travelled and what they saw.

Especially given what they had to work with, which wasn't much. Can you imagine trying to draw an accurate representation of the east coast of Canada or the proportions of the Great Lakes, using nothing but seventeenth-century technology? Champlain did it.

Maps have fascinated mankind since . . . pretty well forever, really. The oldest man-made map we know was not of this earth at all. On the wall of a cave in Lascaux, France, there is a series of dots that astronomers confirm unmistakably charts three bright stars, Vega, Deneb and Altair, as well as the star cluster we call the Pleiades. Archaeologists say the uncannily accurate map was drawn by cave dwellers nearly nineteen thousand years ago. Just think: our ancestors were mapping the night skies nearly ten thousand years before the New Stone Age began.

Nowadays we're all map-makers—or map facilitators, at least. Anybody with a GPS on their dashboard or a smart phone in their pocket can instantly conjure up the coordinates for a ski chalet in the Rockies or a good sushi restaurant in downtown Tokyo.

It's a far cry from the bulky Mercator projection maps that hung off the blackboard when I was a kid. Those things gave most of us our first look at the wide world around us.

Too bad it wasn't an accurate one. School maps altered our perceptions of the planet we call home and they left us with some peculiar ideas. Empires were assigned colours—the British Empire, I recall, was pink. I still think of the long-vanished renegade state of Rhodesia as rose coloured. Other misconceptions abound. The maps depicted Norway and Iceland as almost the size of continents, and Canada, with all those provincial borders slicing north to south, looked like a colossal pink salami.

A clumsily carved pink salami at that. Oh, BC and the Prairie provinces looked neat enough, but then came Ontario with that chunk of gristle hanging off its chin. And the Maritimes? Forget about the Maritimes. Their borders made them look like some preliminary sketch scribbled by Picasso.

The most astounding map I've seen is technically not a map at all. It's a photo taken on December 7, 1972, from the window of the Apollo 17 spacecraft as it whirled through space forty-five thousand kilometres from earth. You've seen the photo. They call it the Blue Marble because that's what the earth looks like—a wispy blue marble hanging against the inky black backdrop of interstellar space.

It's an amazing photograph—perhaps the most amazing photograph ever taken. It changed the way we see ourselves. There are no borderlines on the Blue Marble. Russia is China is the Pacific is Canada is Earth. Everything we've ever known is in that photo. Everyone we know, everyone we hate, and the millions upon millions we will never know. Everyone who ever was and everyone who ever will be. Kings and carnival barkers; cardinals and courtesans. Everything mankind has ever built; everything we've ever sung, painted or written. All of us together, on a glowing blue marble. Our lifeboat in the sea of space.

I hope we've got somebody aboard who knows how to patch leaks.

Weapons of Mass Distraction

You are sitting at a table—sweating, distracted and more than a little edgy—in a slightly skungy downtown San Francisco lounge called Jones. You are with a gaggle of people you've never met before. You are not here for the cocktails or the floorshow or to listen to stand-up comedian hopefuls. You are here for the same reason the others are and none of you is laughing or bantering or looking very happy. In fact you're probably wringing your hands and looking at your shoes right now. You are there because of one simple, ugly truth: you are an addict, a junkie and you are finally ready to acknowledge that you need help. And when your turn comes to speak you hope you will have the courage to stand up and say in a clear, loud voice:

"Hi, everybody. My name is Art and I am a . . . a . . .

"A nomophobic."

Relax, buddy. Everybody at the club tonight is wallowing in exactly the same leaky boat. They are here because, like you, they are addicted—wired, actually—and they're finally ready to admit that their addiction is wrecking their lives.

That's what this get-together is all about. It's billed as a Device-Free Drinks event. The idea is to teach people how to survive without a WMD in their pocket or purse.

That acronym doesn't stand for Weapon of Mass Destruction; it stands for Wireless Mobile Device. These people are going to attempt to spend the next few hours separated from their iPhones, iPads, iTouches, BlackBerrys, Android devices, smart phones or other digital leg iron of choice.

Sounds absurd but it's real enough. An estimated thirteen million Brits suffer from nomophobia—the fear of being separated from their mobile phone. It's even worse on this side of the Atlantic. The average American mobile user is online 122 more hours per year than the average Brit. (That's the best part of a week wasted staring at a little box in your hands.)

A bad habit for sure—but an addiction? Absolutely, according to the experts. A report in a recent issue of *Newsweek* magazine claims that overindulgence in cellphone use, not to mention texting, tweeting and web surfing, can quite literally rewire human brain circuits. Brain scans of adults deemed nomophobic—which is to say people who use their devices more than thirty-eight hours a week—display symptoms that are eerily similar to those found in the brains of cocaine addicts and hard-core alcoholics. Those symptoms range from serious anxiety to clinical depression—even rage or acute psychosis.

This particular Device-Free Drinks get-together at the lounge has attracted about 250 digital junkies and they are offered a variety of diversionary pastimes to help wean them from their toys. There's a glass jar labelled "Digital Detalks" that's full of strips of paper, each one bearing a slightly-off-the-wall conversational opener, such as: "What's the best sound effect you can make?" and "What does your grandmother smell like?"

The idea is to derail your digital brain and rewire it to think outside the WMD box. To help in the weaning process there are a half-dozen twentieth-century digital devices available.

Typewriters by Smith-Corona. The manual kind.

Does it work? One participant says if you can make it through the first twenty minutes without running back to reclaim your checked-in cellphone or iPod, then you've got a chance of reclaiming your life.

But really, it's too early to tell.

Will there be more Digital Detox gatherings like this one in the lounge? You can count on it. Might even be one near you.

If and when it happens, you know how you're going to find out about it, right?

Somebody's bound to post it on Facebook.

Your Call Is Important—Har-Har

As I write, there are an estimated 1.3 million Canadian adults out of work.

I can fix that.

Put them to work, I say. Put them to work at the other end of my telephone line.

There is a galaxy-sized vacuum at the other end of my phone line and it is crying out for human beings to fill it. At the moment it is occupied by a cringe-making mechanical Robovoice. Every time I call my bank, an airline, a government office, the CBC or a large business concern, Robovoice intercepts my call with what has to be the most insincere statement uttered since Richard Nixon's "I am not a crook."

"Your call," purrs Robovoice, "is important to us."

No. No, it's not. If my call was important it would be answered by one of the living, breathing 1.3 million unemployed Canadians out there who could use a warm, comfortable desk job answering phones.

What "Your call is important to us" really means is the exact, 180-degree opposite. It really means, "We've found a way to make even more money by firing our receptionists and replacing them with a recording. Incoming calls are so cosmically unimportant to us we're willing to risk offending the crap out of our customers by forcing them to converse with a vending machine."

What's more, the messages from Robovoice ("This call may be monitored to ensure voice quality"—gimme a break) are so blatantly false they wouldn't bamboozle the most gullible and compliant customer this side of Elmer the Safety Elephant.

We don't all surrender meekly. Many of us instinctively punch "0" the instant we hear Robovoice warming up, and often that will put us in touch with a human operative. As for the more devious and sophisticated "Interactive Voice Response Systems," there is a growing guerrilla network of websites that offers tips on how to sabotage the CCBs (cheap corporate bastards). One website counsels that we should abandon the frustrating practice of mashing button after button ("For help with overbilling, press 368") and just holler "OPERATOR!" at the receiver until a *Homo sapiens* comes on the line. Another website advises us to swear like a paratrooper—apparently X-rated diatribes can trigger emotion-detection technology that brings a live operator on the run.

Feels good, but it's bad for the blood pressure.

Problem is, even if we shout or curse or use technological voodoo to bypass most of the commands, they've still got us dancing like trained monkeys—when all we really want is to connect with another human being with a brain and a heart.

Is that really so much to ask?

We could always take our business elsewhere—providing there *is* an elsewhere. But with businesses going global and conglomerating like cancer cells, too often Robovoice is the only game in town.

My friends say I'm a Luddite when it comes to phone technology. They say I'd be happier if the world communicated by smoke signals.

To which I say: Nonsense. I'm an up-to-date guy when it comes to telephone technology. After all, I do have Call Waiting.

If you call me and you get a busy signal it means you wait until I'm through.

Come On—Get Real!

Human kind cannot bear very much reality.

—T.S. ELIOT

I don't get reality TV.

Oh, I understand why it's popular with television producers and entertainment conglomerates—they get entire TV series delivered to their door without having to pay for writers or expensive studios and sets; they get to use non-union "actors" willing to perform for free or next to it.

But why does anyone want to watch the result?

To see what happens when a gaggle of strangers gets marooned on a desert island? Puh-leeeze. That's no desert island and nobody's marooned. This is a celluloid entertainment, remember? At the bare minimum there's a camera operator, a lighting technician and a sound person riding the levels on hidden microphones. I'm also willing to bet there's a director, an assistant director and a gaggle of college dropout "special assistants" clutching clipboards just off-camera.

Not to mention a helicopter and crew on standby in case somebody wants fresh croissants with their coffee.

It's a shuck, folks—and the French, bless their mercenary hearts, appear to have figured that out. Last year the highest court in France ruled that contestants in the French version of *Temptation Island* were entitled to contracts and employee benefits, including a thirty-five-hour workweek, overtime . . .

And oh, yes. A base pay rate equivalent to nineteen hundred dollars per actor per day. French production company executives sobbed that they'll have to come up with nearly seventy-one million dollars in back pay.

Cry me a *rivière, chéri*. The *Idol* franchise brought in that much in just three months on air.

But when it comes to reality TV, the money is just, well, unreal. Consider the maximally mammaried, minimally talented reality TV star Kim Kardashian. Estimated salary for last year: six million dollars.

And then there's Planet Calypso, a mineral-rich frontier on which investors around the world have been snapping up properties and leases for the past few years. One of those investors, Hollywood film-maker/entrepreneur Jon Jacobs, recently cashed out his Planet Calypso properties for a cool $635,000 US.

Not bad, for an investment of a mere hundred grand.

Especially not bad when you consider that Planet Calypso doesn't exist.

It's an imaginary asteroid, part of an online game called Entropia Universe. Jon Jacobs pocketed more than half a million real dollars by selling fictional real estate on a make-believe celestial body.

As usual, you and I are slightly behind the curve. Planet Calypso is only one of many mythical marketplaces on which online investors are actively "doing business." A marketing firm called In-Stat estimates that online players spent seven billion dollars last year on the purchase of non-existent property and goods.

Which brings us to the Toronto Public Library. Thanks to the introduction of an innovative project, TPL patrons with an active library card can partake of a project called the Human Library. Participants don't take out a book, a tape or a CD; they take out a living, breathing, interacting human being. Some of the people waiting to be "signed out" (for a half-hour at a time, conversation only) include a retired police officer, a comedian, a former sex worker, a model and a person who has survived both cancer and homelessness.

The idea is to facilitate conversations between library patrons and people from other walks of life whom they might not otherwise get to meet. The Human Library is an attempt to "travel back in time," in effect, to an age when, as a TPL official put it, "storytelling from person to person was the only way to learn."

Sounds like a great idea, the Human Library.

No doubt some Hollywood hotshot is figuring out how to turn it into a reality show.

Dear Siri: Please Marry Me

Pssst. You lonely? Looking for a little . . . female companionship? Have I got a girl for you.

She's not cheap, but she's very, very good. Knows how to . . . take care of business, if you get my meaning.

No, I mean really take care of business. She'll call a cab, text-message your kids, book you a table at a good Thai restaurant and make sure you remember your dentist's appointment. When you're heading out the door she'll remind you to take along your wallet, your travel mug and the car keys.

She's sharp, reliable, available 24/7 and what's more she'll never quit on you, no matter how big a jerk you are. If you curse her out, she just tut-tuts and says, "Now, now." If you're a perverted jerk and ask her to "talk dirty" to you, she sighs and says, "Dust. Silt. Gravel. Mud."

And if you really go bananas and start cursing her out she'll say, "How can you hate me? I don't even exist."

Well, yeah . . . there's that.

"Siri," as she's known, is not a living breathing human; she's a voice-activated app that comes along with Apple's iPhone 4S. But she doesn't talk in that familiar, annoying automaton drone we all know from bad movies and our GPS. Siri's voice is unnervingly warm and real. What's even freakier: Siri is actually getting smarter all the time.

Not only are her canned answers updated by Apple experts regularly, Siri can also store the questions to and answers given from her tens of millions of customers and draw on that info to answer your queries. And Siri is fiercely loyal even if it means a walk on the wild side. "Where can I hide a dead body?" one owner facetiously typed. Siri responded with a list of nearby municipal dumps, metal foundries and swamps.

Many customers have come to rely on their new best friend Siri rather a lot. This trend could have been predicted. Last year, Martin Lindstrom, a consumer advocate, recorded the responses of subjects when they heard their cellphones ring. Magnetic resonance imaging detected a frenzy of brain activity, normally associated, says Lindstrom, with feelings of intense love and compassion.

Big surprise. Remember Tamagotchis? Back in the 1990s a craze swept Japan (and eventually much of the world) for a tiny gizmo about the size of a rabbit's foot that you could attach to your key chain. Owners were encouraged to feed, train and even medicate their Tamagotchis every day.

They had to—otherwise the Tamagotchi could sicken and even "die."

This, remember, was not a gerbil, a cricket or a teddy bear. It was an electronic gadget that changed its image depending on what its owner did (or didn't) do with it. Neglect your Tamagotchi even for a few hours and you could come back to find that it had "grown wings" (in other words, died).

Tamagotchis were not remotely human-like, yet many owners developed alarmingly deep personal relationships with them. There were stories of owners attempting to adopt their Tamagotchis as members of the family.

Tamagotchis were a passing fad that waxed and waned, like the hula hoop and Britney Spears. But Siri? I've got a feeling she's going to be around for a while.

Siri's persona is so lifelike, says one customer, "you almost forget that the intelligence we're dealing with is artificial."

That's no big surprise either—but apparently Siri can handle it. She's already fending off marriage proposals.

Yael Baker, a New York media consultant, was so smitten with

Siri's expertise that she impulsively typed, "Siri, will you marry me?"

To which Siri responded, "That's sweet, but let's just be friends."

A Dear John letter from your phone app. How lame is that?

The Father of the Couch Potato

How long have we had TV remotes to play with? Ten years, you figure? Twenty, maybe? You're way off. TV browsers were around before most of the people reading this were born. Before man walked on the moon. Before the Toronto Maple Leafs won their last Stanley Cup, even. We're talking Mesozoic here.

The TV remote has been around since 1955 when a Chicago engineer named Eugene Polley invented it. Polley's prototype wasn't exactly the sleek plastic pellet with eleven dozen buttons that we're used to losing in the sofa pillows nowadays. His invention looked like a ray gun from sci-fi special effects. It had a pistol-grip handle and a trigger and it was called the Zenith Flash-Matic. It wasn't pretty, but it did the job.

Well . . . sort of. Polley's ray gun worked a bit like a flashlight. The viewer pointed it at one of the four corners of the TV screen and pulled the trigger. The top left-hand corner of the screen contained a photocell that would turn the TV on and off. You aimed at the top right-hand corner if you wanted to go to the next channel; the bottom left-hand corner if you wanted to go back to a previous channel; and the bottom right-hand corner if you wanted to mute out what Polley called "those noisy TV commercials."

Or perhaps I've mixed up the corners. A lot of viewers did, which was one big complaint about the Flash-Matic. Another was the fact that the TV photocells frequently reacted with ordinary sunlight to change channels, go on and off, or mess with the volume, all on their own.

It wasn't perfect, but it was revolutionary. Eugene Polley modestly suggested his invention was "the most important invention since the wheel."

Well, hardly—but it was a major influence on television productions and the way we watch the box.

Before Polley's Flash-Matic, viewers who wanted to adjust the volume or change the channel were forced to put their feet on the floor, levitate to a vertical position, walk across the room and interact with the TV manually. Humans, being the lethargic creatures we are, often elected to put up with whatever drivel was emanating from the screen, rather than, you know, actually getting off our lard butts and moving.

The result was some astonishingly mediocre television fare (anyone remember *The Arthur Godfrey Show*?). Eugene Polley's Flash-Matic changed that. It allowed viewers to be discriminating AND lazy. We swiftly developed into a species with the attention span of a fruit fly. Horatio flapping his gums on *CSI Miami*? Zap it in favour of the Nature Channel. Oops, a pollution special—bo-ring! ZAP! Check ESPN. Uh-oh—Jeep commercial. ZAP.

The Flash-Matic is no longer with us, but its heirs and successors are. Back in its day Flash-Matic had to contend with no more than twelve channels, maximum. Today's browsers navigate a universe of hundreds of channels, not to mention computer games, the Internet and our personal music libraries.

No need to get off the couch at all, really. We hardly need our legs anymore. Perhaps over the next millennia or two our DNA will morph and mutate so that those massive, now useless thigh and calf muscles get diverted to where they'd really be of use—in our thumbs.

Eugene Polley won't be there to see it. He died recently at the age of ninety-six, still convinced that he'd made a seminal contribution to human civilization. "The flush toilet might be the most civilized invention ever devised," he told a reporter, "but the remote control is the next most important."

Um, actually Eugene, there are those among us who wouldn't have minded if that first remote control had been accidentally flushed down the first flush toilet.

When Ya Gotta Go . . .

I can't go to the bathroom anymore.

No, no, it's not that. There's nothing wrong with the personal plumbing; it's the public washrooms that don't work for me anymore.

I hail from the horse-and-buggy days of public washrooms. In my day, if you wanted to flush a toilet, you pressed the shiny doohickey on the tank and you were done. To wash your hands, you turned on the hot-water tap (left) and the cold-water tap (right) until an agreeably comfortable flow gushed from the spout and you scrubbed away. Drying the washed hands was a simple feat: a couple of paper towels from the handy wall dispenser would do the trick.

That's not how it works anymore. Approach a sink in a modern public washroom with your hands lathered up in supplication and you trip a sensor—which decides how much water you will get, and what temperature it will be. Usually that means a tepid squirt that wouldn't wash the lint from a gerbil's navel. No matter—your hands are at least dampish now, which means you need some paper towels to . . .

Not so fast, forest killer! Modern public washrooms don't do paper towels. They provide eco-friendly, environmentally responsible sanitary hand dryers that produce warm air to dry your hands.

Theoretically.

The machine wails like a banshee; you look like an idiot trying to shake hands with yourself and your hands remain wet and dripping.

No problem. Now you can wipe them on the inside of your pant legs and creep out of the washroom, trying not to look like a pervert.

Of course I haven't even mentioned those most inconvenient of all the public conveniences—that sombre line of metal stalls ranged against the back wall.

The toilets.

They've been modernized too. Gone is the shiny, manually operated flush lever on the toilet tank. It's been replaced by another sensor. A very sensitive sensor. It responds to your every bodily movement. Thus, when you open the stall door, the toilet flushes. When you take off your jacket, it flushes again. It flushes when you sit down; it flushes when you stand up. The water I waste in one trip to a public toilet stall would probably irrigate a Saskatchewan wheat farm through a drought.

That's one scenario. Often the sensor doesn't work. At all. And you are left with a toilet you would dearly like to flush . . . but there's no flush handle.

Perhaps if you waved your arm. Or your leg. Or both legs and both arms.

This helps to explain those noisy, desperate shuffles you occasionally hear emanating from the stalls of public washrooms. It sounds like some *So You Think You Can Dance* hopeful in there, executing a complicated routine but no, it's just some poor schlub trying to activate a balky toilet stall sensor.

They're not done tinkering with our public toilets either. Toto, a Japanese toilet manufacturer, has unveiled a model they call the Neorest AH tankless toilet. No toilet paper with this baby—instead the "client" is treated to an extremely personal wash and blow-dry all activated by, yes, an unseen sensor. Cost of the Neorest AH tankless toilet? Four thousand dollars.

All so I can experience what happens to my jalopy in a hands-free car wash? No thanks.

I'll just hold it until I get home.

If the Phone Rings, It's Not for Me

People ask me if I have a cell.

Trillions, I think. But I know what they mean. I tell them yes, I have a cell.

Oh, good, they say, and they ask me for the number.

It doesn't matter, I tell them, because I never have my cellphone on.

Then why do you have one, they ask me. So I can call someone if I need to, I say.

But . . . if somebody wants to get hold of you, they can't, they point out.

Exactly, I tell them.

The reason I carry a cellphone is that I'm a geezer who likes to walk in the bush, sometimes on pretty sketchy trails. One of these days I might slide on a root, trip on a rock or fall down a hill. If my luck continues to deteriorate, chances are I'll break something. When that happens (assuming I survive) I'd like to be found by Search and Rescue, not turkey vultures. Ergo, my cellphone. It's for emergencies.

Contrary to popular belief it is not that life-threatening to be "out of touch" with the rest of the world for brief periods of time. Humankind managed brief forays into solitude for millennia before Samsung and RIM and Nokia came along. For most of my life it's been the norm to rely on land lines, Canada Post, a loud wolf whistle or a polite "ahem" when one wanted to make contact with somebody else.

Otherwise, you were on your own.

Nowadays people are seldom on their own except when they're asleep. People check their BlackBerrys in restaurants and theatre lobbies, on buses and subways, in elevators and waiting rooms. When my plane touches down—as soon as the wheels touch the tarmac—there's an in-cabin frenzy as passengers paw for their smart phones to see if they've missed any calls or text messages while they were temporarily aloft and out of contact.

What did they do before cellphones? They thought, I suppose. They daydreamed and fantasized, stargazed and woolgathered.

They retained some mental space in their life.

Seems to be out of fashion now. Recently we had a guest (I'm not naming names but you know who you are) over for dinner and a TV movie. The dinner went well; the movie not so much. Said guest sat hunched over his smart phone furtively text-messaging for an hour and a half.

Such behaviour would have been considered boorish even a decade ago but it's rather commonplace now. People think nothing of being in your company and talking to somebody else who's not present. Weird.

Once I saw a young couple in an intimate bistro sitting at a table adorned with a candle and a lovely white rose in a vase. Very romantic. Except they were not holding hands or murmuring sweet nothings to each other. They were each bent forward, peering into their handhelds and text-messaging . . . who? Who the hell would be important enough to talk to at a moment, in a situation, like that?

How has such a tiny piece of technology come to have such power over us? We should have seen it coming.

More than a hundred years ago, when the clunky old telephone was a brand new invention, a forward-thinking Frenchman had one installed in his château, then invited the painter Edgar Degas to dinner.

He also pre-arranged to have a friend phone him during dinner so that he could impress Degas.

Dinner was served, the phone rang, the Frenchman rose with a flourish and talked on the telephone for a few minutes, then returned, glowing with pride to the table.

"So that is the telephone," Degas said gloomily. "It rings and you run."

Caution: Future Dead Ahead

Nostalgia ain't what it used to be.

—ANON

Indeed it ain't. I've just learned that the Nickelodeon cable network is preparing to launch a new block of programming whimsically entitled "The 90s Are All That."

Yes, it's TV that recycles a decade. No, they're not talking about the 1890s.

I can't even remember the 1990s—and I don't drink or do drugs.

It's not that I'm nostalgia challenged. I feel a distinct sense of mourning for family farms, elm trees, ten-cent coffee and drive-in movies.

I miss milkmen, gas station attendants, paperboys and telephone receptionists.

I long for the heft of a real typewriter, metal hotel room keys, vinyl records—and I'd swap my flimsy plastic cellphone lozenge for a good old clunky rotary job in a heartbeat.

But that's not the world we live in anymore. Today, trends pop up on the far horizon and then disappear with a whoosh in the rear-view mirror before we have a chance to hiccup.

It took Tolstoy six years to write *War and Peace*. The media phenomenon known as "Shit My Dad Says" went from original Twitter feed to YouTube sensation to bestseller to hit TV series in just six weeks. I grant you, in terms of quality there is some distance between the two works, but still . . .

Last year, in a moment of lemming-like consumer delusion, I briefly considered lashing out eight hundred bucks for a brand new state-of-the-art iPad. Good thing I resisted. The launch of the next state-of-the-art iPad earlier this year has rendered the original hopelessly obsolete.

It's not just iPads—have you got an iPod? Put it on eBay, pal. The iPhone was a dagger in the back of the iPod, the sales of which have been sagging steadily for the past three years.

While you're at it, dump your discs. I'm not talking about LPs and 45s—they've been extinct for eons. I mean your floppy discs, your mini-discs, yea, even your CDs and DVDs. iTunes and Netflix are pushing them off the cliff even as I type these words on my laughably out-of-date laptop (two years old and ready for the scrapyard).

Those CDs still make nifty drink coasters, though. And if you string a few of them together and hang them in the garden they might keep the starlings away.

Some old technologies refuse to lie down and die.

Fax machines, those mastodons of office communication, lurk on desktops everywhere—right beside the computers and scanners that were supposed to replace them.

Film cameras are supposed to be dead and buried—the world's last roll of Kodachrome colour film was processed at Dwayne's Photo Service in Parsons, Kansas, not long ago—but diehard purists insist that digital photos lack the "soul" of old-fashioned film. Wishful thinking or not, you can still buy film for your Kodak Brownie.

Back about the time North Americans were first getting used to the idea of telephones and electric lights there lived a nephew of the Sioux warrior Crazy Horse named Red Fox. He was a chief himself, a learned man and an early advocate for aboriginal rights. In his autobiography he wrote: "I met Thomas Edison and Alexander Graham Bell and many others who impressed me as great people, but pride in them and their achievements has not over-awed me, for I am not convinced that the comforts and advancements which they have brought to the world have made people more content and happy than the Indians were through the centuries on the mountains, prairies and deserts of the primeval, virgin continent."

A few years ago a tourist in Washington, DC, was riding in a taxi past the National Archives and noticed the legend carved in granite across the front of the building. It read: "WHAT IS PAST IS PROLOGUE."

"What does that mean?" the tourist asked.

"It means," said the driver, "that you ain't seen nothin' yet."

I fear that both Chief Red Fox and the Washington cabbie were right.

Hears to Us

*I'm sixty-six, I don't have perfect hearing, and if I listen
to loud music or go to gigs I do tend to get tinnitus.
DON'T WE ALL????*

—PETE TOWNSHEND, ON HIS BLOG

I read that trivia pearl to my partner. She grunted, "So what's your
excuse?"

That's a two-pointer in my household. She not only nailed me for
being hard of hearing, she managed to work in a reference to my lame
guitarsmanship. She's good.

But she's at least half-wrong. I'm not deaf. I went to an audiologist
and had myself checked out. "Your hearing is excellent for someone
your age," she said. I told her my partner wouldn't agree. The audiologist smiled and said, "Well, there is a phenomenon known as 'selective
hearing.'"

Related THAT little nugget to my partner. Two-pointer for my
side. I think.

As for Pete Townshend, he is the poster boy for self-inflicted
hearing loss. Pete's in the Guinness World Records for being onstage
at what's been called "the loudest concert ever," at a London football
stadium in 1976. Add to that his years of playing lead guitar for The
Who, standing between amplifiers as big as boxcars and cranked to the
max and yeah, it figures that Pete might have hearing issues from time
to time.

For most of us the fear of going deaf is only a notch down from the fear of blindness but a lot of hearing-challenged humans have done all right. Thomas Edison had serious hearing problems but managed to invent the light bulb, the phonograph and over a thousand other devices. Lou Ferrigno, a.k.a. the Hulk, has impaired hearing. So do Halle Berry and Rob Lowe.

Musicians seem to be particularly vulnerable. Aside from Pete Townshend, Brian Wilson of the Beach Boys and George Martin, the famous Beatles producer, did some of their best work under an aural handicap.

Can you imagine trying to create classical music with faulty hearing? Fauré did. So did Boyce and Smetana. The great Beethoven went deaf as a kumquat but went right on composing masterpieces—even though he would never hear a single note of them.

According to the Public Health Agency of Canada, 30 percent of us over the age of sixty-five will experience hearing loss, but it probably won't be Ludwigian in scope. For most of us it will be grumbling about those news announcers who all seem to mumble the news, or wondering why cocktail chatter has turned into a wall of sound.

Not catastrophic. More . . . amusing.

A man sees me straining to follow conversation in a restaurant and says, "You should get a hearing aid like mine. Light as a feather; almost invisible. Cost me twenty-five hundred bucks."

"Really," I say. "What kind is it?"

The man says "Half-past four."

Two Winnipeggers bump into each other at the corner of Portage and Main, the coldest crossroads in Canada. "Windy, isn't it?" says one.

"No," says the other. "I'm pretty sure it's Thursday."

"Me too," says the first guy. "Let's go grab a beer."

Making light of a disability—blasphemous? Nah, laughter's always good for what ails you.

I say: "Hear, hear."

The Good Old Hawking Game

Remember the last NHL lockout/strike/labour action/five-on-five power play? The one that went on for umpty-seven consecutive weeks?

A nation yawns.

It is hard to work up enthusiasm over a back-alley donnybrook in which millionaires face off against billionaires. Vincent Lecavalier, captain of the Lightning, a team that plays out of that hockey hotbed Tampa Bay, didn't get paid during the lockout but he's probably got enough stuffed under the mattress to get by. Vincent has an eighty-five-million-dollar—yes, you read right, an $85,000,000—contract to chase a rubber disc in various arenas for the Lightning until 2019. He's by far the best-paid NHL-er but the rest of the players aren't living on table scraps. The average salary tops out at just under 2.5 million simoleons a year.

I stopped seriously following NHL hockey about four decades ago when the average salary was twenty-five thousand a year. Star players like Bobby Hull and Gordie Howe did better—they were up in the hundred-thousand-a-year range—but tears must cascade down their heavily scarred cheeks when they hear that today the most tangle-footed, knuckle-dragging bench-sitting goon in the league makes twenty-five times as much as they ever did.

How can NHL owners shovel out that kind of money for salaries and still manage to be rolling in dough? The answer's a simple one: advertising. In 1972 all teams in the NHL played on a rink surrounded by blank white boards and the single sponsor was Imperial Oil. Check those boards now. They are festooned and bespackled with ads for insurance companies, hockey gear manufacturers, banks, mortgage firms, department stores, beer, deodorants and cough medications. Likewise, the telecasts are splattered with ads for everything from snow tires to potato chips.

That's why each year media moguls go into vicious feeding frenzies trying to outbid each other for the privilege of putting hockey on TV—and by extension into the living rooms of millions of hockey fans, a.k.a. consumers.

The fans pay the ultimate price and not just for the blitz of blurbs, plugs, jingles and thirty-second spots that plague the at-home viewer—those ads dictate the pace of the game. First-time attendees at a live NHL game are often stunned at how often the on-ice action is unexpectedly halted for several minutes, during which the players from both teams skate around in aimless figure eights, waiting for a daisy chain of TV commercials to cycle through the broadcast.

The NHL holds no monopoly on hockey advertising. During the aforementioned hockey lockout a photo in the sports section of my newspaper showed Boston's Joe Thornton streaking up the ice, but not in a Bruins uniform. Instead he was wearing the colours of HC Davos, a European pro team based in Switzerland. Thornton, along with dozens of other locked-out NHL-ers, was trying to stay in shape by playing overseas for the duration of the lockout.

But it's not Thornton's uniform that caught my eye—it's what was plastered all over Thornton's uniform. Advertisements. I could decipher logos on his skates, on his hockey stockings, his hockey pants and gloves. There were at least a dozen ad patches on his hockey sweater and undoubtedly more on the back of it. His helmet carried a banner flogging Skoda automobiles. Thornton looked like he just skated through a garbage bin full of advertising flyers.

Ironically, in the same issue there was a picture of Paul Henderson holding up the hockey jersey he was wearing when he scored the most famous goal ever—the one that gave Team Canada its triumph over the Russians back in 1972. The jersey features a large red abstract leaf,

Henderson's number, 19, the word CANADA—and that's it. No ads, not even Henderson's name.

But that was four decades ago. Back when hockey, not advertising, was the name of the game.

My Name Is Art. I Am a Shopaholic

The year's still young, but I'm putting my money on James Livingston for Bonehead Title of the Year.

Mr. Livingston has penned an article for *Wired* magazine called "Against Thrift: Why Consumer Culture Is Good for the Economy, the Environment, and Your Soul."

Pow! As titles go, that's right up there with "The Leadership Genius of George W. Bush."

Livingston enjoins his readers to "ignore what the economists, journalists and politicians would have you believe . . . Go to the mall and knock yourself out."

Or you could just wait until the Visa or MasterCard bill comes in at the end of the month. That'll knock you out.

We live in the age of *Homo consumeris*. Our highest civic calling is to buy junk we don't need with money we don't have. Our day of worship is, well, every day, really, but our High Holy Day is Black Friday, that twenty-four-hour feeding frenzy just after American Thanksgiving, when shopping malls and big box stores slash their prices and, in anticipation, salivating shoppers mass at the doors like hordes of Visigoths at the gates of Rome.

On a recent Black Friday a shopper in Los Angeles pepper-sprayed fellow shoppers in order to get at discounted Xbox consoles. A riot broke out and blood was spilled over two-dollar waffle irons in Little

Rock, Arkansas. And a woman was shot near a Walmart in Myrtle Beach, South Carolina, as she carried her goodies to her car.

The insanity continued right up until Christmas Eve, when Nike put its latest line of retro basketball shoes on sale. Police had to be called in more than a dozen cities, including Charlotte, North Carolina, where shoppers smashed glass doors to get at the product.

We're talking about running shoes, folks.

Somebody once said, "The American consumer is not notable for his imagination and does not know what he 'wants.'" Maybe not, but he wants it now, and money is no object.

Those Nike shoes? Two hundred dollars a pair.

We're still talking about running shoes, folks.

There are one or two beacons of hope in the blitzkrieg of berserker bargain hunters. For one thing, the thrift stores are thriving. People from all walks of life, unmoved by advertising campaigns to buy fifty-dollar T-shirts, one-hundred-dollar warm-up vests and, yes, two-hundred-dollar sneakers, are heading down to the thrift shops to get barely used goods at a fraction of the mall price. The proceeds from the thrift stores I frequent go to the local hospital and to a women's shelter. Where's the downside?

Another ray of hope comes from Elvis Costello. The famed musician (and husband of jazz diva Diana Krall) made the news recently when he publicly urged his fans NOT to buy his latest CD/DVD compilation.

Why? Too expensive, that's why.

Costello says the price tag of two hundred dollars "is either a misprint or satire."

"All our attempts to have this price revised have been fruit-less," says Costello on his website (www.elviscostello.com/news/steal-this-record).

But if you really want to get a very special CD for your sweetie, Elvis has some helpful advice. "We can whole-heartedly recommend *Ambassador of Jazz*," says Elvis. "It contains TEN re-mastered albums by one of the most beautiful and loving revolutionaries who ever lived—Louis Armstrong."

"Frankly," adds Costello, "the music is vastly superior."

When's the last time an advertiser advised you to buy his competi-tor's product—because it was better?

Finally—truth in advertising. Good on ya, Elvis—see you down at Value Village.